Not

Free

Not Slave, Not Free

The African American

Economic Experience

since the Civil War

Jay R. Mandle

Duke University Press   1992   Durham & London

© 1992 Duke University Press
All rights reserved
Printed in the United States of America
on acid-free paper ∞
Library of Congress Cataloging-in-Publication Data
appear on the last printed page of this book.
Chapter 1 is a revised version of "Black Economic
Entrapment," reprinted from *The Meaning of Freedom:
Economics, Politics, and Culture After Slavery*, edited
by Frank McGlynn and Seymour Drescher, by
permission of the University of Pittsburgh Press. © 1992
by University of Pittsburgh Press.

Contents

Tables

Preface

When I wrote in 1978 *The Roots of Black Poverty: The Southern Plantation Economy since the Civil War*[1] I wanted to account historically for the fact that the incomes received by African Americans were disproportionately low. To try to understand why that was so I asked the question why the black population remained resident in the South, the least-developed region in the United States, as long as it did. In addition, I inquired about the strategies the African American population adopted in attempting to overcome its economic difficulties. In effect, these remain the questions I address in this new work as well.

An examination of the citations in this book compared to those in *The Roots of Black Poverty* will reveal that the postbellum South has continued to be the object of a dramatic outpouring of scholarly work. Important books have been written by at least a half-dozen scholars, while the number of journal articles on the subject is prodigious. Many of these efforts dramatically improve our understanding of the South's economy after the Civil War. I hope that it will be apparent to the reader who compares this book to *The Roots of Black Poverty* that my own understanding of the dynamic of black and southern life has become more incisive as a result of my grappling with the conclusions and data generated in the recent literature.

Nonetheless the fact remains that the problem of the historical source of contemporary African American poverty still has not received the attention it deserves. It is at least arguable that poverty among African Americans more than any other concern represents the central domestic issue in American political life. Yet there remains a gaping disjuncture between the writing of black history and analyses of the contemporary economic condition of the African American population. Among contemporary scholars only a few authorities follow the lead of William Julius Wilson in attempting to link contemporary problems with their historical antecedents.[2] Thus it is that I decided to write a second book on the historical origins of African American poverty. On one hand I think there remains a need for this kind of historical analysis. On the other hand the recent literature on the subject has been substantial enough for me to reconsider and re-formulate my understanding of the relevant issues.

Readers will see that now, as in the earlier book, I follow Edgar T. Thompson and the plantation school generally in arguing that the social dynamic associated with the plantation way of life set off the South from the rest of the country. African American poverty cannot, I think, be understood unless it is placed in the context of the peculiar institutional setting that is associated with the plantation way of life.

While acknowledging that specific intellectual debt, it would be impossible to try to thank all those who have contributed to the evo-lution of my thinking on this subject during the last thirteen years. No listing could possibly be complete. Yet those who have been closest to me over this period of time have contributed the most. It therefore would be evidence of a lack of gratitude not to identify Joan D. Man-dle, Jon Mandle, Iz Reivich, Paul Lyons, Lou Ferleger, and my now deceased parents, Abe and Bella Mandle, as the individuals who have helped me the most to wrestle with the intellectual problems and is-sues raised in this study.

Introduction

This study explores the reasons for the disproportionate poverty that afflicts the black population in the United States. Such an explanation requires a historical account. Contemporary patterns are the product of the historic past; present-day change is influenced by the trajectory that historical experience imparts. As a result without an examination of how today's situation developed it is not possible to understand the reasons for, much less remedy, black economic deprivation.

That the African American population in 1989 was poorer than the rest of the population in the United States is clear. Per capita income for blacks in 1989 was $8,747, only 58.7 percent of the white per capita income for that year. Black household income too fell short; the median level of $18,083 was 59.5 percent of the same statistic for whites. Whereas 43.2 percent of black households received under $15,000 in 1989, only 25.3 percent of whites received this low level of income. Perhaps the most graphic and troubling set of statistics to be reported is that in 1989 43.7 percent of black children (individuals under eighteen years of age) lived in households which received income below the officially defined poverty level—$12,675 for a household of four people. The corresponding figure for the white population was 14.8 percent.[1]

The economic history of the black population cannot be studied without taking into account the wider society of which this group is a part. It is necessary to understand the role African Americans played in that wider context and how that social structure influenced the opportunities available to blacks. In this study the task is complicated by the need to examine two different social and economic contexts. Before World War II the nature of southern society and the role played by blacks in that region is the focus of attention. Thereafter, because of the migration of the black population from the rural South, attention shifts to the problems and opportunities which confront African Americans in urban settings.

The interaction between regional economic development and the economic status of African Americans in the South is a central theme in this study. On one hand the general degree of development present in the region was a major determinant of the level of income which African Americans could earn. On the other hand the extent to which blacks were afforded the opportunity to employ and develop skills in production affected the pace of the South's economic development more generally.

That the South was the least developed part of the United States during the years in which African Americans predominantly were rural residents there was fundamental in accounting for the low income levels they received. Of course, it was true that even within the constraints imposed by southern underdevelopment, racial discrimination meant that black incomes were lower than they could and should have been. Nonetheless southern underdevelopment was fundamental in dictating that black income levels were low.

But causality worked in the reverse direction as well. The process of modern economic growth is closely associated with the emergence of productive competencies among the population. Primarily this occurs through formal education and schooling, although skills are enhanced through work as well.[2] If, however, a society limits the capabilities of or options available to a substantial fraction of its population, it is likely that its own level of economic development will be lower than it otherwise might have been. In turn, of course, this will result in lower levels of income received by the population.

Indeed my argument is precisely that the way black labor was used in the South of 1865 to World War II, as well as in urban areas generally between World War II and the present, resulted not only in low levels of income received by African Americans, but also significantly retarded southern economic growth and urban development in turn.

The first five chapters of this book concern the black experience in the South and the remaining chapters address black economic participation in urban America. Chapters 1 through 3 focus on the aftermath of slavery in the South and the process by which the region's plantation economy was reestablished on a non-slave basis after emancipation. In this, attention is directed to racially discriminatory hiring in the North as an important mechanism in bottling up black labor in the plantation South. The constrained opportunities available to the former slaves, although functional for the region's plantation economy, go a long way to account for their poverty in this period. But chapter 4 then argues that in turn southern economic underdevelopment was itself the consequence of that plantation economy.

It was this self-reinforcing mechanism of deprivation and underdevelopment, as argued in chapter 5, that made the South a distinctive and economically backward region.

Chapters 6 and 7 examine the pattern of migration of the African American population during the twentieth century. Although migration was important at the time of World War I, the evidence suggests that not until World War II did it become sufficiently massive to effect substantially black incomes or the nature of Southern society. With the migration of the 1940s and 1950s, however, a fundamental transformation occurred. As the rural South was vacated by blacks, plantation agriculture was denied the abundant labor essential to its viability. The labor scarcity which resulted from black migration in turn triggered the mechanization of southern agriculture and became an important element in the emergence of the South as the most rapidly growing region in the country during the years after World War II.

Chapter 8 focuses attention on the black economic experience once the rural South was vacated. The legacy of life in a plantation economy manifested itself in cities and contributed substantially to black poverty there. In particular the weak development of black entrepreneurship and professional attainment, which deprived blacks of important income-earning opportunities, is directly attributable to former conditions in the rural South. Rapid economic growth in the 1950s and 1960s, nonetheless, permitted a substantial degree of occupational integration to occur, resulting in substantial income gains by blacks in these years. The slowing of growth in the 1970s, however, reduced the pace at which African Americans continued to progress, all the more so because a lag in the education of blacks compared to whites put the former at a disadvantage in the labor market. That very educational deprivation in turn seems to have been an important element in accounting for the reduced rate of economic growth in the United States generally. Today the United States' economic growth remains stuck at unsatisfactorily low rates, while black incomes and educational attainment too remain far below desirable levels. While it is true that slow growth has meant that black economic progress has been less than it would have been if economic expansion had remained at a high level, a hopeful message does emerge from this study. An increase in the education and skills of the black labor force might, if put to use in the United States economy, not only raise the incomes of African Americans but also result in a higher rate of economic growth for the nation as a whole.

Reestablishing
the Plantation Economy

1

The New World system of slavery was the result of the coerced emigration of people from Africa. Between the sixteenth and the middle of the nineteenth century the number of such forced relocations is thought to be about ten million.[1] It was in the eighteenth century that the enslavement of Africans reached a peak, with about 60 percent of the forced emigrations occurring in that century. Most slaves were transported to Brazil and the Caribbean. Only about 6 percent of the total slaves were transported to the United States. However by 1825, because of favorable demographic circumstances, 36 percent of all slaves in the Western Hemisphere were living in the United States. As Robert Fogel and Stanley Engerman put it, "despite its peripheral role in the Atlantic slave trade, the U.S. was, during the three decades preceding the Civil War, the greatest slave power in the Western world and the bulwark of resistance to the abolition of slavery."[2]

There were some slaves present in the North, particularly in New York, during the seventeenth and eighteenth centuries, but even in these colonial years slavery was predominantly a southern institution.[3] At the time of the first national census in 1790 nearly all of the roughly 750,000 African Americans resident in the United States were slaves, almost all of whom lived in the South. By 1860 the African American population had risen to about 4.4 million, more than 90 percent of whom resided in the South and nearly 90 percent of whom were slaves.[4] Concentrated initially in the Chesapeake Bay area, slaves were reallocated in association with the spread of cotton cultivation to the South and the Southwest. By 1860, 46.3 percent of the African American population resided in the states of the South Atlantic region, 31.4 percent in the East South Central states, and 14.5 percent in the West South Central, with the remainder thinly distributed throughout the rest of the country.[5]

The force used to transport people from Africa meant that labor was supplied to producing units in the New World in numbers greater and at costs lower than would have been the case if voluntary labor had been recruited. Fogel and Engerman estimate that such labor savings to cotton producers in the United States totalled more than 50

Table 1 Regional Per Capita Income as a Percentage of National
Per Capita Income, 1840–60

	1840	1860	Change
Northeast	134.4	141.4	7.0
North Central	67.7	69.5	1.8
South Atlantic	68.8	65.6	−3.2
East South Central	71.9	69.5	−2.4

Source: Calculated from Robert William Fogel and Stanley L. Engerman, *Time on the Cross: The Economics of American Negro Slavery* (Boston: Little, Brown and Company, 1974), vol. I, p. 248.

percent of what otherwise would have been their wage bill.[6] Furthermore slavery permitted cotton plantation owners to achieve economies of scale through the use of gang labor, facilitating the development of large units of production. These favorable production conditions were combined with a buoyant international demand for cotton. As a result, the slave-based cultivation of cotton was profitable for nineteenth century planters.[7]

It is possible to compare the performance of the economy of the slave South with that of the rest of the United States using the estimates of regional per capita income available for the years 1840 and 1860 (Table 1). What Table 1 seems to suggest is that the per capita income in the South under slavery approximated that of the agricultural North (cited as the North Central states in the table), but that it lagged seriously and increasingly behind the Northeast—the region where industrialization had taken root. Such a pattern is consistent with the analysis contained in Fogel and Engerman's work which emphasizes the productive capability of slave labor, but also acknowledges that slavery militated against industrialization.[8]

The Emancipation Proclamation and the South's loss in the Civil War represented, of course, a major discontinuity in the region's historical experience. With these events southern slave owners had irretrievably lost their property rights in persons. According to estimates prepared by Roger Ransom and Richard Sutch for five southern states (Alabama, Georgia, Louisiana, Mississippi, and South Carolina), the market value of slaves in 1860 had accounted for nearly 60 percent of the total amount of capital invested in agriculture and was an amount far in excess of the total investment in manufacturing

present in those states. As such emancipation represented an enormous loss to the planters.[9]

The experience of slaveholders in the southern United States
was similar to that of planters elsewhere in the New World when
emancipation was imposed on them. Everywhere emancipation occurred the potential for economic catastrophe faced the former slave
owners. Deprived of their most valuable asset sugar planters in the
Caribbean in 1838, like cotton planters in the South in the 1860s,
confronted the need to reorganize their production processes or face
bankruptcy. In light of the profundity of the crisis they faced it is
remarkable how successfully the planters accomplished the necessary
transition to a post-slave organization of production. With the ex-
ception of Haiti the ending of slavery typically did not mean the demise of the planter class. Plantation owners in most cases were able
to accomplish the transition from what Gavin Wright calls laborlords
to landlords, and in the process continue in their former role as the
dominant class in society.[10]

Critical to planter persistence was a mechanism to supply the
plantations with the abundant, reliable, and inexpensive labor that
slavery had provided. Such a mechanism could take one of two forms.
A new labor force, one specifically tied to plantation work, might be
recruited. Alternatively the plantations might benefit from obstacles
confronted by the former slaves in their search for nonplantation
employment opportunities. If nonplantation employment were not
available, the ex-slaves would be compelled to supply their labor to
the planters at low wages, thereby providing the workers essential for
continued plantation viability.

The first option was employed in Trinidad and Guyana. Because
these British colonies possessed abundant unutilized land the former
slaves, with freedom in 1838, were able to vacate the plantations in
large numbers and establish themselves as peasant proprietors. For
those who chose to continue to work on the estates the resulting labor
scarcity resulted in an upward bidding of wage rates to the point that
many former slaves were able to make land purchases themselves.
The planters responded to the resulting crisis in their way of life by
initiating a scheme, in concert with the colonial power, to import a
new population and labor force. These new workers, largely from the
Indian subcontinent, were indentured to plantations thereby ensuring
continued plantation productive capability. Even so the process of
substituting indentured workers for slaves was not an easy one and

it was not until the 1870s that the planters in these colonies were fully able to replenish their stock of labor from overseas and establish conditions of labor abundance. Once that was done, however, the bargaining power that the former slaves had been able to exercise in the determination of wages was undermined. Similarly with the reviving of profitable production on the estates the availability of plantation land for sale to peasant cultivators disappeared. Thus by the 1870s or 1880s the growth of an independent West Indian peasantry, and the options which that growth represented, slowed considerably. The region's sugar plantations were able to restore their once jeopardized hegemony.[11]

In the "closed resource" islands of the Caribbean the threat to plantation dominance represented by emancipation was more easily contained. That on an island like Barbados or the smaller Windwards and Leewards very little land was not already controlled by large plantations meant that the opportunity to escape plantation life and attempt to become an independent peasant cultivator was largely preempted. Juridical freedom did not provide the former slaves with widening employment opportunities. Because squatting was not feasible the plantations did not confront a dramatic reduction in their labor supply or increased wages. As a result after only a short period of adjustment plantation agriculture became reinvigorated and continued in its hegemonic economic status.[12]

The U.S. South had to face many of the same problems confronted in the Caribbean. There, as in the West Indies, the ending of slavery raised the question of the terms upon which the former slaves would make themselves available for work on the plantations. The greater the range of employment options available to the freed persons, the more demanding those terms would be. Conversely a failure to find substantial employment off the plantations would mean that the planters would hold the upper hand in determining the conditions of post-Civil War employment.

Certainly there was one alternative that likely would have put an end to the plantation way of life. Providing land and the resources necessary to enable the former slaves to become commercial farmers would have thoroughly revolutionized the southern social structure. And in fact, based at least in part on actions adopted by the Union army, the ex-slaves believed this is what would occur. In June 1863 federal troops in Clark County, Alabama allowed the ex-slaves to measure off and occupy their former master's land.[13] In 1864 Sherman's troops also told the former slaves that land would be made available to them. Indeed Sherman's Special Field Order No. 15, issued in January 1865, created a reserve of land for the exclusive use of the former slaves. According to this order forty acres were to be allotted to each family, with horses and mules to be loaned to them as well. In addition, according to Claude Oubre, the initial circulars and orders issued by the Freedmen's Bureau "convinced freedmen that they would receive land." Oubre, in this regard, quotes an assistant commissioner of the bureau as telling a convention of blacks that "they must not only have freedom, but homes of their own, thirty or forty acres, with mules, cottages and school houses."[14]

But neither the slaves, the army, nor even the Freedmen's Bureau would be decisive on the question of land reform. The decision whether to confiscate planter land and provide it to the former slaves was to be made in the Congress. There, led by Thadeus Stevens, a small group of Republicans struggled in favor of such a program and, Eric Foner reports, as the war progressed their support grew. Confiscation was defended as the only means to break the power of the southern plantocracy and as the only means to create a new class of black and white property owners who would provide a new foundation for southern society. Foner writes that this view could be defended as "the corollary of a traditional widely shared value—the conviction that democratic institutions must rest on an industrious middle class." Thus Stevens and his associates attempted to appeal to generally accepted values within the Republican party in advancing the argument for a program of land confiscation and redistribution to the former slaves.[15] In this regard the radical Republicans in the United States seem to have sought more from emancipation than did English abolitionists. W. A. Green writes that the latter judged the success of abolition not in terms of changing the social system in the colonies, but rather "in terms of the ability of emancipated labour to preserve and enhance existing plantation economies."[16]

While the idea of providing land to the former slaves was consistent with at least some of the values which animated the congressional Republican party, the problem was that taking land from the planters was in conflict with another, more deeply felt, set of principles. For fundamental to the world view of many who were opposed to the southern way of life was the belief that free labor should rise or fall only according to the diligence of its effort. In this perspective the risk in giving land to the former slaves was that the government would indicate, in the words of *The Nation,* "there are other ways of securing comfort or riches than honest work." Similarly the *New York Times* argued against confiscation because it would violate "the fundamental relation of industry and capital. . . . An attempt to justify the confiscation of Southern land under the pretense of doing justice to the freedmen, strikes at the root of all property rights." Thus congressional Republicans were caught between their commitment to property rights and their hostility to southern planters. Having deprived the planters of what the Republicans viewed as illegitimate property in persons, northern politicians could not bring themselves to deprive them of what were acknowledged to be legitimate property rights in land. Although Foner writes that as late as the spring and summer of 1866 confiscation was still a contentious issue, the congressional discussion was its high-water mark and a radical land reform never came close to implementation.[17]

While land confiscation was being debated and defeated Congress did pass the Southern Homestead Act. Introduced in January 1866 and passed in June of that year, this law specified that in the distribution of southern public land, homesteads should not be allotted to southerners who had taken up arms against the North. At the same time, the fact that the land allocations were relatively small in size was understood to mean that the South would not become attractive to northern whites or European immigrants. In effect, therefore, this legislation was designed principally to benefit former slaves. As the chair of the Senate Committee on Public Lands put it at the time, "the object of the bill is to let them [the blacks] have land in preference to people from Europe or anywhere else."[18]

The problem was that the land in the public domain was generally of poor quality. The best land in the South had long since been put into private cultivation. As a result, according to Christie Pope, heavy capital expenditures and labor were necessary for cultivation to be successful on the land which remained. But it was precisely capital which the former slaves lacked. As a result, according to the Freedmen's Bureau reports, only about 4,000 freedmen had made homestead applications by October 1869. As Pope writes, "despite the fact that the bill was passed expressly for the benefit of freedmen, only an insignificant percentage of the four million Negroes in the South were able to take advantage of the law."[19] The failure of land reform and the ineffectiveness of the Southern Homestead Act meant

Table 2   Value of Property Holdings by Race: Arkansas, Georgia, Louisiana, North Carolina, 1880–1910 (in dollars)

State	1880	1890	1895	1900	1910	Change*
Arkansas						
Whites	—	—	267.53	247.80	307.39	39.86
Blacks	—	—	29.96	33.15	49.14	19.18
Georgia						
Whites	285.40	455.19	—	386.23	413.78	128.38
Blacks	8.00	17.46	—	16.62	26.59	18.59
Louisiana						
Whites	—	294.67	—	300.82	401.41	106.74
Blacks	—	16.46	—	14.86	16.31	−0.15
North Carolina						
Whites	—	241.64	—	241.70	304.27	62.63
Blacks	—	14.07	—	19.01	33.12	19.05

Source: Georgia: Robert Higgs, "Accumulation of Property by Southern Blacks before World War I," *American Economic Review*, vol. 72, no. 4 (September 1982), p. 720; Arkansas, Louisiana, North Carolina: Robert A. Margo, "Accumulation of Property by Southern Blacks before World War I: Comment and Further Evidence," *American Economic Review*, vol. 74, no. 4 (September 1984), p. 770.

*Figures represent data over different time periods for different states: Arkansas, 1895–1910; Georgia, 1880–1910; Louisiana and North Carolina, 1890–1910.

that an overwhelmingly large proportion of the African American population remained landless.

This absence of land reform meant that land ownership was impossible for the vast majority of the former slaves. Robert Tracy McKenzie has estimated that in the postbellum period in order to have purchased forty acres and a mule "a sharecropper would have had to save annually ten percent of his net income—a doubtful possibility in itself—for eighteen consecutive years."[20] Some were able to do so but these were the exceptions: most could not.[21] Under these circumstances it is no surprise to learn that black property holdings stood at levels far below that of whites in the South. Data compiled by Robert Higgs and Robert Margo for four southern states between 1880 and 1910 are reported in Table 2. What is obvious in this table is the vast gap in the ownership of wealth by race present in this period in the region. Whereas, for example, white wealth in 1900 ranged between $241.70 and $386.23, the range for blacks was between $16.62 and $33.15. Obviously compared to whites the black population was impoverished.[22]

Indeed Steven DeCanio's econometric analysis provides empirical support for the view that only a program of land redistribution could have resulted in a substantial narrowing of this black-white wealth differential. After reviewing the results of his model of wealth accumulation, DeCanio concludes that "emancipation without property condemned the blacks to a lengthy period of economic disadvantage." According to him "even if all markets had operated perfectly and no discrimination had been practiced against the freedmen either in wage payments or in their access to occupations, this initial gap in tangible capital would have produced by itself most of the gap in income between blacks and whites throughout the late 19th and early 20th centuries."[23]

As a result of the limits to black land ownership the planter class was for the most part able to retain ownership of plantation land in the postbellum South despite the substantial losses in wealth experienced as a result of slave freedom.[24] This retention meant that in the largely agrarian southern society the former slave owners as a group were able to retain their positions of economic and social importance.[25] Their continued control of land meant, in addition, that they were the persons from whom the former slaves would have to seek employment if they were to continue to work cultivating cotton. For as Gerald David Jaynes writes, "given that the federal government chose not to deliver land to the freedmen, the only avenue open for them was to enter some form of contractual arrangement with the reinstated owners of the land."[26]

Southern planters replicated efforts made in the Caribbean to augment the region's labor force through immigration, although their attempts were not as successful as those in the West Indies and Guyana where colonial policy was supportive of such efforts. States such as South Carolina, Louisiana, Alabama, Arkansas, Mississippi, Tennessee, Texas, and Virginia all passed laws to encourage immigration, sent immigration agents to other countries, or set up immigrant agencies. Initially the intent was to import Chinese to replace African Americans on the plantations, but efforts were also made to recruit migrants from Europe and from among new arrivals in the North. Generally, however, these efforts were unsuccessful. According to

Roger Shugg some Chinese were brought from Cuba and the Philippines, but they ". . . soon deserted the plantations to become independent fishermen and truck farmers for the New Orleans market." Similarly the effort to use "Coolie labor failed because wages in railroad construction were higher than the income which could be earned in Southern agriculture."[27]

Thus in the absence of a program of land redistribution or substantial immigration to the South the former slaves and the plantation owners confronted each other in the labor market. What emerged was a system of plantation tenantry, in which compensation was made in the form of a share of the crop. With sharecropping, plantation owners provided cultivators with tools and equipment as well as access to land to be cultivated by the cropper and his family. In share tenantry the tenant provided equipment and perhaps work animals for production.

In the southern context a substantial degree of landlord control was retained in both sharecropping and share tenantry. Although the revenues generated on tenant plantations were shared between the planter and tenant according to a contract entered into at the beginning of the crop year, managerial prerogatives, with their attendant social consequences, remained with the planter. It was the planter who made the decisions concerning crop choice, methods of cultivation, and the financing and marketing of the crop. Although the sharing of the risks associated with variations in output and price was implicit in the share contract, the management decisions concerning those risks were left, unilaterally, in the hands of the planter. Thus although sharecroppers possessed more discretion in the allocation of their time than did members of work gangs, much less slaves, they nonetheless continued to be subject to planter authority. As Jaynes has written, "the southern sharecropper bore all the burdens of an entrepreneur but was dispossessed of freedom of choice in making managerial decisions."[28]

Joseph Reid, Jr. argues that what emerged was a mutually satisfactory accommodation. Reid's view rests on the assumption that because "slaves did not learn many managerial and marketing skills" the "freedmen were woefully unprepared to farm on their own." As a result the former slaves could not have been able satisfactorily to fill the role of farmer-manager. What was required by the freed persons, according to this view, was training in those areas in which they were deficient. According to Reid this is precisely what sharecropping did. For in this tenantry system "the offer to landlords of shares of the crops by these new black and white tenants promised to secure landlords' assistance and thereby to make tenants' prosperity quick and sure." As seen by Reid sharecropping was in the economic interest of both owner and tenant. According to him not only is it the case that generally a "knowledgeable landlord will want share tenants." It also is true that "somewhat unknowledgeable but ambitious farm workers will be share tenants."[29]

Intriguing though it is, Reid's hypothesis that sharecropping was the farm arrangement of choice for both planters and farm workers is untenable. No observer doubts that what the former slaves wanted was landownership. Indeed Foner explicitly rejects Reid's view of sharecropping. Foner writes, "The desire to escape from white supervision and establish a modicum of economic independence profoundly shaped blacks' economic choices during Reconstruction, leading them to prefer tenancy to wage labor and leasing land for a fixed rent to sharecropping. Above all it inspired the quest for land of their own."[30] With regard to the former slave's preference for landownership, Vernon Wharton has written that "their very lives were entwined with the land and its cultivation: they lived in a society where respectability was based on ownership of the soil; and to them to be free was to farm their own ground."[31] Not only did land represent a means to attain social status, it also represented the most obvious strategy for escaping poverty. That such a reallocation of land away from the planters and to the newly freed black population did not occur probably was more important than any other event in determining that poverty would be the fate of that population in the years after the Civil War. It is of course possible to argue, as Reid perhaps would, that the former slaves were economically irrational in their preference for an owner-occupier status. But arguing in that way requires the assumption that the people involved do not know their own best interests, an assumption which generally is inadmissable in the kind of analysis presented by an economist like Reid. Furthermore a very different picture from Reid's emerges from the records of the Freedmen's Bureau as reported by Jaynes. In his account the planters sought to restore as much of their lost authority as possible while continuing to possess a stable labor force throughout the crop season. On the other side the former slaves resisted such planter efforts. Their intention was to provide as much content as possible to their new status as freedpersons. In the absence of landownership they sought to avoid gang labor and to exercise as freely as possible their new-found right to be mobile. With regard to the latter Jaynes writes that the former slaves preferred wages to a share system so long as those wages were paid at frequent periodic intervals. In this regard Jaynes quotes an Alabama planter as saying that the former slaves preferred wages to share tenancy "because, like regular soldier or college boys, they don't want the trouble of balancing chances and precasting [*sic*] the future." To this Jaynes adds that the preference for wages was not only because of the desire to avoid risk, but also that "short term wage contracts offered the greatest independence to workers." With wages, Louis Manigault wrote in the 1870s the former could avoid "being bound down to the same plantation all the year round."[32]

The planters too might have preferred a wage system. Available evidence suggests that wage-paying plantations were substantially more efficient than those organized on a share basis. However neither the former slaves' preferences nor the planters' desire for efficiency was realized in this regard. This failure occurred because the planters lacked access to sufficient credit to finance a wage system. Such a secure source of financing is required if a routine payroll is to be met in an industry where revenues from sales are generated only once a year. As Jaynes writes, "the true legacy of federal agrarian policy in 1865 was the failure to provide the financial assistance to southern agriculture that would have allowed a restructuring of a sounder credit policy."[33]

But more than a simple reallocation of land would have been necessary for a land reform program to have been successful in overcoming black poverty. To make land reform a viable strategy the government, in addition to providing land to black cultivators, would have had to ensure the former slaves access to the credit necessary to finance the production of the staple. In addition new cultivators would have required efficient transportation and access to markets as well as technical information on seeds and fertilizers. If these requisites had been satisfied then the extent of the prosperity resulting for individual black farmers would have depended on such factors as entrepreneurial talent, the strength of the agricultural markets, and soil quality.

It seems reasonable to speculate that in such circumstances the pattern of black income would have been different from the virtually uniform poverty that affected African American sharecroppers after the Civil War. In all likelihood the opportunity to generate and share in property income in cotton or some other crop would have resulted in the emergence of significant income differentials within the black population. In this the more competent, better-endowed or more fortunate black farmers would have prospered and the contrary would have been the case for those less well positioned. But what seems clear is that many more southern African Americans would have emerged from this process as wealthy business persons than was the case in the plantation economy. With land provided to the former slaves, in short, the nearly universal poverty experienced by the black population would have been absent. The result would have been a distribution of income resembling that of the white farmer population. That is, with land redistribution and the financial and technical assistance essential for the success of such a program, the economic position and welfare of the black population might have become comparable to that of the population of the country as a whole. Its failure and the continuation of the southern plantation economy meant that the persistence of the differential economic experience which has characterized the white and black populations in the United States was allowed to continue and draw new life.

Despite the fact that the absence of a radical land reform prevented black commercial farmers from developing in large numbers, the goal of landownership and through such ownership the establishment of a class of black business persons remained integral to black economic strategies. Thus August Meier, in his discussion of black thought in this period, cites as representative a statement issued by a national convention of black leaders meeting in 1897: "We are to a great extent the architects of our own fortunes, and must rely mainly upon our own exertions for success." The statement went on to recommend that "the youth of our race [adopt] a strict morality, temperate habits and the practice of the acquisition of land . . . and advancing to mercantile positions and forcing their way into various productive channels of literature, art, science, and mechanics."[34]

Racial solidarity was an integral part of this approach. Because there were relatively few business opportunities for blacks in the South given the plantation economy structure, it was important under this strategy for black consumers to patronize black businesses. One African American lawyer at the same convention cited by Meier put it this way: "We must help one another. Our industries must be patronized and our laborers encouraged. . . . We are laboring for race elevation and race unity is the all important factor."[35]

Table 3   Black Farm Owners as a Percentage of Black Farmers in
Plantation States, 1890–1910

	1890	1900	1910
Alabama	13	15	15
Arkansas	24	25	23
Georgia	13	14	13
Louisiana	18	16	19
Mississippi	13	16	15
South Carolina	21	22	21
Total	16	17	17

Source: Loren Schweninger, *Black Property Owners in the South, 1790–1915* (Urbana and Chicago: University of Illinois Press, 1990), table 10, p. 164.

The ultimate expression of the concept of self-help came later in the century from Booker T. Washington. Washington believed that southern African Americans should deliberately refrain from political participation and, at least in the short run, accommodate themselves to the southern social structure. He believed that on the immediate agenda of the southern black population should be learning skills and entering trades in order to compete economically. In his view only with an increase in productive competence would African Americans be able to attain and satisfactorily employ their constitutional rights. Washington was a leading proponent of establishing industrial schools for blacks and was at the forefront of a movement to endow such schools with philanthropic funding. According to Meier what Washington had in mind was "developing a substantial propertied class of landowners and businessmen."[36]

The fact is, however, a substantial class of black landowning farmers failed to materialize and it was this failure which doomed the strategy of self-help in the South. Table 3 reports that between 1890 and 1910 the number of black farmers who owned their own land hovered between 16 and 17 percent with no upward trend evident. At the same time, as Loren Schweninger notes, most black farmers in what he calls the "Lower South" controlled "very small amounts of property." W. E. B. DuBois' study of the wealth held by black farmers in Georgia in 1899 indicated that 68 percent of those farmers controlled land assessed at less than $200.[37] With regard to black landownership in the South generally, Schweninger writes that "considering the political, economic and institutional barriers they faced, the prejudices of whites and the general backwardness of the South itself, it is not surprising that most Negroes remained landless."[38] In fact roughly 83 percent of black farmers remained landless in 1910; in the absence of a governmental program of land reform, transactions in the market did not result in the emergence of a broad-based class of African American owner-occupiers in southern agriculture.

Two consequences flowed from the limited emergence of a black farmer-owner class. The first was that overwhelmingly the African American population in the South was denied entrepreneurial experience and therefore the opportunity to develop managerial and business skills. Share tenancy did not provide such an opportunity. Under the terms of the tenancy contracts employed in the South, managerial decisions were left exclusively in planter-owner hands. At least in terms of assessing market conditions and choosing patterns of production, share tenants were employees not managers. Sharecroppers were not entrepreneurs.

The second consequence was that the poverty experienced in the plantation context constrained the development of black businesses. Given the size of the African American population and its concentration in the South, it was at least a plausible strategy to urge black consumers to patronize black business. At the same time, however, African American consumers tended to be impoverished. Therefore although racial solidarity might ensure the availability of a market for businesses owned by African Americans, it was a constrained market. Failure to transcend this constraint doomed a business to a limited scale. But of course a search for a market among white consumers tended to be doomed by the race prejudice present in the region. The South's plantation economy, in short, was distinctly inhospitable to nurturing black business.

The success of a self-help strategy of economic advance such as Washington advocated ultimately depended not only on African Americans successfully endowing themselves with skills, but also on the creation of opportunities for the skills to be put to profitable use. But the difficulty was that the limited availability of those opportunities were the consequence of the very plantation economy in which they found themselves. To achieve changes in that social organization implied the use of political means—a strategy Washington explicitly ruled out.

There was, in short, an assumption, almost certainly unwarranted, that underlay the single-minded focus on the self-help strategy: once blacks were properly socialized and endowed with appropriate skills the structure of the southern economy was sufficiently flexible to accommodate upwardly mobile individuals. This may have been the case for a few. But in the plantation economy, if the hope was that through such means the widespread poverty among southern blacks was to be alleviated, that assumption was probably incorrect. Equipping southern blacks with the skills to allow them success as commercial farmers did not mean that any more good land would be available to them.

The emphasis on uplift and on the development of a class of black businessmen characteristic of Washington's thought has been interpreted as a kind of black nationalism.[39] Indeed on at least one occasion Washington himself asserted, "We are a nation within a nation," and like other advocates of self-help he encouraged black patronage of black business establishments.[40] Yet it is important not to confuse a concern for the emergence of black businesses and farms with the advocacy of political separation and self-government, normally the salient characteristics of nationalist movements. For self-help represents a response to imposed separation and stands as a strategy to achieve advances within that structure. Nationalism, on the contrary, sees separation and self-rule as its goals. These ends were not Washington's.

It was DuBois who saw that preparation alone was insufficient to achieve economic advance. DuBois believed that economic advance could not be achieved without a political counterpart. As a result he vigorously opposed Washington's view that a low priority should be attached to contesting the electoral disenfranchisement by African Americans in the South. DuBois argued that it was "utterly impossible" to create a class of black businessmen and property holders who could defend their gains without the right of suffrage. He maintained that Washington's desire for thrift and self-respect was at variance to his counsel of "silent submission to civil inferiority," because such self-denial was "bound to sap the manhood of any race in the long-run." DuBois believed, in opposition to Washington, that failure to participate in the struggle for political rights undermined the chances of achieving and sustaining precisely the kinds of self-help programs which Washington defended. The ballot, DuBois believed, was the least "a guilty nation could grant a wronged race," and "the only method of compelling the South to accept the result of the Civil War."[41] DuBois, in short, continued the call for the dismantling of the plantation economy and with it the ending of the subordination of African Americans essential to plantation agriculture's viability.

The Limits to African American Freedom

2

Central to the viability of plantation agriculture is the availability of a large number of workers at low wages. For such labor supply conditions to prevail, the options available to plantation workers must be severely constrained. Only if their choice of work is narrow do individuals accept the kind of arduous and low-paying job which plantation labor typifies. In the United States for most workers most of the time such conditions did not prevail. Long-term economic growth in the years after the Civil War meant that the demand for labor generally was strong and employment options therefore were wide. As a result wages in the United States were relatively high. Yet it is my argument in this chapter that for the black labor force confinement more than opportunity characterized the labor market. As a result the South's plantation economy was able to survive through the second half of the nineteenth century and about a third of the twentieth century.

Sharecropping was not slavery. Sharecroppers and tenants could, if they chose, seek new employers. The occurrence at the end of each crop year of a considerable turnover in plantation tenants suggests that a fundamental advance in employment choice had been experienced with emancipation.[1] In this regard Gavin Wright has convincingly argued that within the South a labor market for black workers was operative. He cites as evidence of the functioning of such a regional labor market high rates of migration from relatively low-wage to relatively high-wage regions within the South and the fact that these differences in compensation tended to narrow over time. Wright is quick to acknowledge, however, that these indicators "do not say that southern laborers were treated fairly or munificently."[2]

But establishing that a black labor market was operative in the South—that is, that slavery had ended—is to cast only partial light on the question of the extent to which the African American labor force in the years after the Civil War could properly be characterized as free. Freedom is always a matter of degree. What is of interest is the extent to which market participants are able to exercise occupational and industrial choice in employment. Freedom for African

Americans after the Civil War, then, should not be defined simply by the existence of a market for black agricultural labor in the South. Instead freedom should be measured by the extent to which African Americans, like other individuals in the country, were free to seek out and secure employment in industries other than cotton cultivation and in regions other than the South.

Gerald Jaynes argues that it is wrong to describe black labor in the postbellum South as free precisely because the compensation system associated with sharecropping and share tenantry immobilized plantation workers for most of the crop year. Because of what Jaynes calls "the long pay"—the delay of compensation until the end of the crop year—the cropper could leave an employer only by forfeiting the compensation to which he or she was entitled, which was received only at the time of the harvest. Thus except for the period at the end of the crop year, sharecropper mobility came at the cost of foregone income for which the cropper had already performed work.[3]

At the end of the crop season, however, a cropper could, and often would, change employer. Even then, however, a second source of immobility was imposed by sharecropping. This source stemmed from the credit relationship embodied in sharecropping. In order to be offered employment on plantations, would-be tenants were required to demonstrate their credit worthiness to prospective landlords.[4] In an environment in which African American agricultural workers were subjected to a withering racial animus, credit worthiness required a reputation for deference as well as productivity. There was a need to be known as reliable and appropriately respectful if an African American were to come to terms with a planter. This dual criteria—productivity and deference—made it important that aspiring croppers' personal characteristics be known and this in turn meant that they could not move to areas where their reputations did not precede them. Typically, therefore, as Ronald Davis puts it, "the average black family moved from place to place, from landlord to landlord, and even from supplier to supplier without ever leaving the neighborhood."[5]

To argue that sharecropping inhibited mobility during the crop year, however, does not speak to the question of why, at the end of the harvest, the plantation workers did not secure employment outside of cotton cultivation. One traditional explanation of the relative immobility of southern black labor has hinged on the question of debt peonage. Peonage exists when a planter forbids the cropper from leaving the plantation because of debt. According to Pete Daniel, ''by 1901 southern society had reached the point where a debt-labor system characterized by violence and corruption or acquiescence of local police officers was openly tolerated.''[6] Daniel does not attempt to quantify the extent of such peonage; however, Michael Wayne's examination of tenant turnover on four Adams County, Mississippi plantations between 1871 and 1874 found that only 19 of the original 42 tenants were still resident at the end of the three-year period.[7] As Wayne himself acknowledges it is difficult to evaluate the representativeness of these data. But the magnitude of the mobility they suggest raises a serious question about the economic significance of the peonage system in constraining the movement of labor.

Debt peonage thus seems to have been relatively ineffective in confining large numbers of individual croppers to specific plantations. Nonetheless when the annual process of sorting out residences and work places was completed, the industrial structure of the black labor force looked much as it had before with little, if any, movement out of the southern plantation cultivation of cotton. Intra-regional mobility was present, even as inter-regional mobility remained at low levels. It is important, therefore, to know what forces, market or otherwise, were responsible for the persistence of southern black laborers in plantation work, even though they moved from one plantation to another.

A free labor force—one able to exercise choice among a wide array of options—would be expected to become widely dispersed among new opportunities. Subject only to the constraints of individual preferences and the matching of skills to those required in the new employment opportunities, the exercise of choice should be associated with a decreased concentration in employment. In the case of the postbellum black labor force, if freedom were operative it should have been associated with a reduced presence in southern agriculture.

But in fact what is salient about the postemancipation experience of African American labor is when measured by geographic, industrial, or occupational dispersion very little change was experienced. Thus, for example, between 1870 and 1910 the proportion of the African American population resident in the South remained virtually stationary, standing at 91 percent in the earlier year and 89 percent in the later.[8] An absence of data makes it impossible to estimate the extent of change which occurred in the industrial structure of the African American labor force in the years immediately after slavery. But as late as 1910 87.8 percent of the African American labor force in five cotton-growing states worked in agriculture and domestic and personal services.[9] Occupationally as well these years saw little change in the African American labor force. In their sample of counties in the cotton South, Roger Ransom and Richard Sutch estimate that only 3.5 percent of the black labor force was in skilled crafts—a figure they contrast with the 5.6 percent of slaves they estimate filled such occupations in 1860.[10] Thus in the decades before World War I, despite the organizational changes that occurred in southern agriculture, not much had changed for black labor geographically, industrially, or occupationally.

Within the plantation South occupational mobility was limited by the difficulty southern blacks experienced in gaining access to productive land and by the slow pace of industrialization in the region. As shown in Table 7 landownership of blacks in the parts of the South dominated by plantations was highly restricted even when compared to other sections of the region. Thus Wayne, in discussing Natchez, Mississippi, reports that most blacks ". . . were unable to make significant strides toward landownership and genuine economic independence. . . . Thirty five years after the war, the number of freedmen and their descendants who owned land in the district was still insignificant."[11] This limited success in gaining access to land in the plantation belt was obviously the consequence of both discriminatory practices in the sale of land and the inability of blacks to raise the funds necessary to purchase valuable black belt property. Their combined effect was to help confine African American workers to the status of plantation laborers, rather than to open up independent commercial farming as an occupational alternative.

Similarly industrialization in the South provided little opportunity for blacks. In the first place manufacturing employment grew only slowly in the region. Between 1890 and 1910 such jobs increased by 5.6 million in the United States, but only 381,000 of these were located in the six states where plantation agriculture was most important—Alabama, Arkansas, Georgia, Louisiana, Mississippi, and South Carolina.[12] Furthermore by no means were all of these nonagricultural jobs open to black labor. As Wright reports "the southern industrial workplace was highly segregated and the lines of segregation were remarkably persistent through good times and bad." In the region's most rapidly growing industrial sector, cotton textiles, only 8.6 percent of the labor force in 1890 was black, prompting Wright to remark that this industry was "the most lily-white of them all."[13] Thus it is clear that because regional industrialization was slow and the black labor force confronted a powerful color bar, new sectors of nonagricultural employment in the South provided only a limited opportunity at best for blacks to escape the confines of plantation life. One obvious source of continuity in the black economic experience is that nonagricultural employment opportunities in the South grew only very slowly, and in many of those which did emerge African Americans were excluded on the grounds of their race.[14]

Over and above these limitations in the South itself black economic immobility prevailed because northern employment opportunities were not filled by migrating southern African Americans. Black net migration from the South to the rest of the country remained at relatively low levels from 1870 until the 1910–20 decade. It was not until World War I that the percentage of the black population resident in the South started to decline at a substantial pace. If an alternative way of life were not available in the South, it also was the case that in the half century after the Civil War a new way of life in the North was also not experienced by the black population. Thus a key to the source of black economic continuity after emancipation rests in the North as well as in the social structure of the South.

Black geographic immobility prevailed despite intense northern demand for labor in these years. Between 1870 and 1920 immigration to the United States averaged in excess of 500,000 per year, an inflow largely representing a response to the growing demand for labor present in the industrial North. Very few northern employment opportunities, however, were filled by migrating blacks (See Table 4). This failure requires an explanation. The North's per capita income was roughly twice the level that prevailed in the South, making it a potentially attractive location for employment.[15] Thus the question which arises is why southern blacks did not become part of the growing northern industrial labor force in these years.

Three different explanations have been suggested to account for the industrial and geographic immobility experienced by black labor after the Civil War. Each isolates one aspect of labor market processes. Thus Gavin Wright identifies information and its costs, Richard Vedder and his colleagues emphasize the preferences of the workers themselves, and Brinley Thomas highlights discrimination in the North. Although strictly speaking none of these hypotheses necessarily

Table 4   Black Migration from the South and Net U.S.
Immigration, 1870/80–1920/30

	Southern Black Migration (thousands)	U.S. Immigration Rates (per 1,000 population)
1870–80	60	5.1
1880–90	70	8.0
1890–1900	168	3.7
1900–10	170	6.5
1910–20	454	3.2
1920–30	749	2.8

Source: U.S. Bureau of the Census, *The Social and Economic Status of the Black Population in the United States: An Historical View, 1790–1978,* Current Population Reports, Series P-23, no. 80 (Washington, D.C.: GPO, n.d.), table 52; Lance E. Davis et al., *American Economic Growth: An Economist's History of the United States* (New York: Harper and Row, 1972), table 5.1.
Note: The correlation coefficient between black migration (x) and international migration rates (y) is 0.73, statistically significant at the 0.05 confidence level.

stands in contradiction to the others (northern discrimination could have existed even if black laborers lacked adequate information about conditions in the North and preferred living in the South) it is important to identify the relative weight to be assigned to each. For choosing among these hypotheses also goes far in answering the question of how much freedom black labor possessed. If, for example, African Americans stayed in the South by choice, immobility could not be considered as evidence of a lack of freedom. On the other hand if northern discrimination were identified as responsible for immobility, such stability would be considered evidence of constrained choice.

The explanation of limited mobility offered by Wright is that "the South was consumed by the turbulence of war and Reconstruction at the very time that mass immigration was becoming an established part of the northern social fabric." The question of timing is important, Wright argues, because "there are strong tendencies to persistence of labor market flows and linkages once begun" and that "the existence of a first wave of migrants from a country is the most important single factor in generating the second wave." In this account, then, "trust among kinfolk" provided the information flow which facilitated the movement of European migrants to the United States North. In the absence of such an information network, migration from the South did not materialize before World War I. That the South did not experience a labor flow to the North in the 1840–70 period is Wright's explanation of why it did not do so subsequently. Because the South did not experience a first round of migration, its labor market effectively did not become integrated with the market in the North.[16]

This explanation of the pattern of migration to the United States North is, however, not consistent with the empirical evidence. Contrary to the anticipation generated by Wright's hypothesis, the region of origin of migration to the United States did not remain stable during the period in question, but in fact changed dramatically. In the years between 1871 and 1890 the countries of northwestern Europe were the dominant sources of migration to the United States, contributing 72.5 percent of the immigrants to the country in those years. A decided alteration occurred after 1890, however. From negligible numbers in the early period, Poland and Central Europe became important countries of migrant origin as early as the 1880s, and were joined by eastern Europe and southern Europe in the 1890s. These regions contributed half the inflow to the United States in the 1890s and 70 percent in the 1900–10 decade.[17]

That the source of immigration was not continuous but experienced abrupt change casts grave doubt on the adequacy of Wright's hypothesis. Wright argues that what was decisive in the South's failure to contribute a population flow to the North was that it had not done so at an early period. But central, eastern, and southern Europe had not done so either and they, unlike the South, became major sources of migrants in the twenty-year period before World War I. Clearly factors in addition to timing must be taken into account in explaining the failure of southern emigration and the discontinuity which existed among regional labor markets.

Richard Vedder and his colleagues similarly are skeptical that information and search costs "alone can explain the paucity of migration out of the South in the first half century after Emancipation or that these costs suddenly or dramatically fell to start the exodus of blacks from the South." Instead they posit a hypothesis which is nothing if not innovative. They suggest that "Southern blacks in the postbellum period genuinely preferred the Southern environment to any alternative. . . ." The authors believe that the "Southern way of life" in which the region's salubrious climate was decisive, made the region "appealing" to the black population. Specifically their view is that "Southern Negroes preferred the relatively warm region of their birth to other regions."[18]

To test this hypothesis the authors employed a model of migration. Using census data they found the following statistical associations: (1) southern blacks had a statistically significant greater tendency to remain in their state of birth than whites or nonsouthern blacks; (2) in the early years after emancipation southern blacks were significantly less prone to migration than northern blacks; (3) by 1920, compared to 1880 or 1900, the greater tendency among blacks to remain in the state of their birth disappeared. All of these conclusions the authors believe support their thesis concerning the strength of the black affinity for the southern climate.[19]

Remarkable as their conclusion appears to be it rests on an elementary, but fundamental, error in method. In reporting the results of their empirical work the authors not only indicate the nature of the statistical relationship they found, but also employ language suggesting causality. This set of claims however is not warranted. Instead of indicating that there was a statistically significant tendency in 1880 and 1900 for southern blacks to remain more than other Americans in their state of birth, the authors write there was a "statistically significant tendency for southern blacks *to want to remain* in their state of birth more than other Americans."[20] Adding the words "to want to remain" in this context is without an explicit theoretical or empirical justification and in no way is motivated by the statistical associations which the authors found. In fact the evidence provided is consistent not only with the hypothesis advanced by the authors, but also with other interpretations. They could be viewed as supportive of Brinley Thomas' thesis that the reason blacks remained in the South is that they were discriminated against in the North. Unfortunately Vedder, et al. do not provide us with any reason for preferring their explanation to the alternatives.

Thomas' hypothesis of racial discrimination in the North is the third explanation available to account for the reason blacks failed to move from the South. As we have seen in Table 4 there was an inverse relationship between black migration from the South and European migration to the United States. As Richard A. Easterlin notes, "immigrants and nonwhites were to some extent substitute sources of labor." The same point is made by Thomas when he writes that "within the unskilled sector there was a high degree of competition between the Negro and immigrants from South Eastern Europe."[21]

Thus the explanation of why African Americans remained in the South may lie in the answer to the question of why European immigrants secured northern jobs, but southern blacks did not.

It seems plausible to argue that in the immediate aftermath of emancipation the former slaves may not have possessed adequate information concerning employment opportunities outside of the South. Slavery had meant precisely that job search was not possible, and as a result channels of information undoubtedly were poorly developed. Thus with freedom it might be anticipated that the new-found mobility of the African American population would be exercised narrowly, in a geographically circumscribed area. But with the passage of time the handicap of inadequate information must have declined; there was limited South-to-North black population movement, which undoubtedly increased knowledge concerning labor market conditions in the North.

A further indication of knowledge of employment opportunities present among southern blacks was the effort of state legislatures in the region to staunch the flow of such information. Antienticement and antirecruitment legislation indicates a concern which would not have been present unless significant numbers of black workers were evidencing an interest in securing employment elsewhere.[22] These took two forms. First, several southern states such as North Carolina, Alabama, Georgia, and South Carolina passed "false pretense" laws. The purpose of these laws was to keep agricultural laborers on the plantations for at least the duration of their contracts. Second, "antienticement" laws were designed and passed to minimize efforts by potential employers to seek out such workers. To prevent or reduce active recruiting of black laborers—especially by industrial entrepreneurs from the North—states such as Alabama, Georgia, Mississippi, and South Carolina passed legislation to prohibit the "enticing" of croppers from their employers. According to Oscar Zeichner, in order to minimize recruitment from the North, the plantation states of Alabama, Georgia, Mississippi, and South Carolina "placed prohibitory restrictions upon employment agents who solicit and send labor out of the states."[23] In addition recruiters were subject to annual licensing fees at both the local and state levels and in some cases were required to post a bond to cover the debt owed by the laborers they recruited. Zeichner summarizes his review of these laws by concluding that "the laws dealing with labor contracts, false pretenses, emigrant agents and the enticing of laborers have assured the planter of legal support in his effort to secure a stable labor supply during the agricultural year."[24]

However, the response of the southern black population to the curtailing of international migration at the time of World War I is the most convincing indicator that the black population possessed considerable insight into the dynamic of the northern labor market. It furthermore suggests that the control associated with antirecruitment and antienticement legislation was relatively weak. Once the movement of labor from Europe was disrupted because of the war, the flow of labor from the South surged. The population-weighted black emigration rate from the states of Alabama, Georgia, Louisiana, Mississippi, and South Carolina in 1910–20 was almost three times the level in 1900–10.[25] As Karl Taeuber and Alma Taeuber report, black age-specific migration rates during this period, in particular for the age category 15–34, "are almost beyond belief."[26]

The inference to be drawn from this episode is that the African American labor force did not lack either information or the desire to move North. Furthermore the growth in black wealth in this period, although considerable when expressed in percentages, was not of an absolute magnitude sufficient to produce by itself such a dramatic change in migration patterns.[27] What seems to have occurred is that with Europeans no longer available, the black population moved with alacrity to respond to the demand which in the past had been satisfied by international migrants. In short the pattern of European employment domination in the North does not seem to be supply-side determined.

No systematic investigation has been made to identify the reasons for the preference of northern capitalists for European rather than southern black workers. Robert Higgs, however, has provided evidence that such discrimination was in fact practiced. Higgs has carried out two statistical tests of discrimination in the setting of wage rates of European immigrants on the one hand and for African Americans on the other. In both cases Higgs allowed literacy and the ability to speak English to be an index of skill. He found that variations in these two variables accurately predicted differences in observed wages among immigrants, tending to suggest that discriminatory practices were relatively unimportant in determining immigrants' wage rates. On the other hand a similar test of black wages in 1909 found that these same indicators of skills predicted wage rates substantially above the level actually paid. This result is consistent with the hypothesis of racial discrimination in the setting of wage rates for blacks.[28]

Stanley Lieberson has provided important corroborative evidence in this regard. He writes, "there is no rigorous study that I know of which examines employers' attitudes toward blacks and SCE [southern, central, and eastern European] groups, but the evidence I have patched together seems to indicate a more favorable disposition toward the latter." In this regard he cites survey data from the 1920s which ranked racial groups on a continuum from "good" to "bad" and found blacks at the bottom of the list. In addition a survey carried out in Minneapolis at about the same time found that "the vast majority of employers surveyed indicated that they would not employ blacks if any were to apply." A president of a steel company is cited as saying that "it would be better . . . if the mills could continue to recruit their force from [Europe]. The Negro should remain in the South." Lieberson comments that what seems to have happened is that an etiquette or set of norms developed among whites concerning the proper behavior of blacks. It defined "black efforts to reach equality as inappropriate." He goes on, "this emphasis called for blacks to remain in their status. . . ." whereas, in contrast, European immigrants were expected to achieve upward mobility. Lieberson concludes that there is "no way of avoiding the fact that blacks were much more severely discriminated against in the labor market and elsewhere."[29]

Similarly, the Philadelphia Social History Project found that in the late nineteenth century "race proved more powerful than the rules that governed spatially conditioned job access." Hershberg, et al. report that blacks "had few manufacturing jobs, even though they lived within easy access to more jobs of this type than any other ethnic group." These authors write that "although the typical black in Philadelphia worked within one mile of 23,000 manufacturing jobs—half again as many as were accessible to the typical Irish, German or native-white worker—he was refused employment." As a result of this refusal blacks ". . . were marginal to the rapidly industrializing urban economy of the period and were considerably more segregated than white immigrants."[30]

Thus it is that neither of the two alternatives which would dramatically have altered the role played by the black population in the United States came to fruition. The former slave population became neither a landowning class of farmers nor a northern urban working class. Instead the largest fraction of this group was left to seek its livelihood as nonlandholding agriculturalists—primarily sharecroppers—still overwhelmingly resident in the South. The foreclosing of alternatives meant that after emancipation, as before the ending of slavery, the role of the black population remained different and separate from that of the rest of the population in the United States. Unlike other groups the range of employment opportunities available to the black labor force was narrowly constrained. Freedom for African Americans therefore was subject to many more obstacles than was the case for other population subgroups.

Tenant Plantation Agriculture

3

The limited occupational choice available to black labor after the Civil War meant that in large numbers African Americans were compelled to work on the South's plantations. In the historical literature, however, the full implications of that confinement have not fully been appreciated. Instead of viewing the limits of black occupational choice as providing the basis for reestablishing plantation agriculture, many scholars argued that what had occurred was the creation of a black peasantry. Thus Roger L. Ransom and Richard Sutch write that "one of the most dramatic and far-reaching developments of the post emancipation era was the decline of the plantation system of agriculture and its replacement by tenant farming."[1]

One reason for underestimating the persistence of plantation agriculture lies in the data collecting methods of the United States Census Bureau before 1910. In censuses prior to that date, the Census Bureau considered each tenant farm in the South as a separate entity. Because of this, census data seem to suggest that a peasantry had emerged replacing the old plantation system. As Roger Wallace Shugg in 1937 wrote, "because land rented by share croppers was put in the same category as farms owned outright, and the several tracts held by a planter were not registered as a single unit, it appeared that peasants rather than peons had taken the place of slaves."[2] But counting each tenant farm separately, in the words of C. O. Brannen in 1924, "fails to represent properly the nature of the plantation." For though postbellum plantations were organized on the basis of a complex system of tenantry, "in matters of administration, supervision, marketing and the like, the plantation as a whole employing tenants or croppers is only one farm."[3]

In the 1910 census, however, the Bureau of the Census altered its data collecting methods and acknowledged that southern tenant farms were part of larger production units. As part of the census of that year, the bureau undertook a special study of plantation agriculture in 325 rural counties in 11 southern states. It is this source which provides our first comprehensive data on the relative importance of plantation agriculture in the region in the postbellum period.

Table 5   Improved Land in Southern Plantation Farms by State, 1910

Location (# of counties)	Acres
Alabama (47)	3,028,979
Arkansas (23)	1,054,049
Florida (1)	47,577
Georgia (70)	2,855,402
Louisiana (29)	1,190,599
Mississippi (45)	3,196,834
North Carolina (21)	530,830
South Carolina (35)	1,652,865
Tennessee (11)	449,506
Texas (41)	1,752,524
Virginia (2)	77,198
Total (325)	15,836,363

Source: U.S. Bureau of the Census, *Plantation Farming in the United States* (Washington, D.C.: GPO, 1916), table 14.

The Census Bureau, however, was not completely clear concerning the basis upon which a county was included in the plantation grouping. It reported instead that ". . . in the great majority of the counties for which plantation statistics are presented the Negro constituted at least half of the total population and that, on the other hand, there are comparatively few counties outside of the area for which plantation statistics are presented in which the proportion is as high as 50 percent." The Bureau was quite explicit in acknowledging that share and tenant farming was the new organizational basis of plantation farming. A tenant plantation was defined as ". . . a continuous tract of land of considerable area under the general supervision or control of a single individual or firm, all or a part of such being divided into at least five smaller tracts, which are leased to tenants." On this basis it affirmed that its study included all counties in the South ". . . in which the plantation system is extensively developed."[4]

The Census Bureau study identified 39,073 plantations in 1910 in the counties under investigation (see Tables 5 and 6). Of these plantations 28,290, or 72.4 percent, were in the six states of Alabama, Arkansas, Georgia, Louisiana, Mississippi, and South Carolina. There are no data presented on the relative importance of plantation agri-

Table 6   Improved Land in Southern Plantation Farms by State, 1910 (in percentages)

Location (# of counties)	%
Alabama (47)	38.2
Arkansas (23)	39.4
Florida (1)	26.2
Georgia (70)	37.1
Louisiana (29)	39.3
Mississippi (45)	47.9
North Carolina (21)	19.6
South Carolina (35)	30.8
Tennessee (11)	23.7
Texas (41)	20.0
Virginia (2)	14.9
Total (325)	33.4

Source: See Table 5.

culture compared to other forms of farming by state, but the study indicates that 33.4 percent of the improved agricultural acreage in the counties of the eleven states studied was in plantations. In the six states mentioned above plantation acreage as a percentage of improved land came to 47.9 percent in Mississippi, 39.4 percent in Arkansas, 39.3 percent in Louisiana, 38.2 percent in Alabama, 37.1 percent in Georgia, and 30.8 percent in South Carolina. Mississippi and Alabama ranked highest in the absolute number of acres in plantation agriculture. The former had about 3.2 million acres in plantation cultivation and Alabama had about 3.0 million acres. These two states alone accounted for almost 40 percent of the total plantation acres reported in the study. Plantation acreage in Alabama, Arkansas, Georgia, Louisiana, Mississippi, and South Carolina accounted for 82.1 percent of all plantation acreage.

With tenant farming their organizational basis, southern plantations typically were divided into two sections—one farmed directly by the owner or manager, and the remainder cultivated by the tenants. The 1910 study found that there were 398,905 tenant farms on the 39,073 plantations investigated, an average of a little more than ten tenant farms per plantation. What the Census Bureau called "landlord farms" were much larger than tenant farms. Average acreage for the former was 330.0 acres in contrast to 38.5 acres for the latter. At the same time, however, improved landlord acreage came only to 86.6 acres compared to 31.2 for the tenants. By multiplying average acreage per tenant by the number of tenants per plantation, and then dividing that number by the total acreage per plantation under cultivation, we learn that tenants were responsible for about three-fourths of the plantation acreage cultivated.[5]

Although the names of the individual counties under consideration in the study were not provided by the Census Bureau, a map of the area containing all 325 counties was provided. By comparing this map with county maps of the states involved, it is possible to identify the specific counties studied. Of the plantation counties, 270 were in the six states mentioned above, plus North Carolina. The remaining 298 counties in these states then formed a grouping of geographically similar, but nonplantation counties, to which the plantation counties can usefully be compared. (See the appendix for an enumeration of these counties.)

Writing in 1924 Brannen reports that the plantation counties include "a considerable part of the most productive and highly developed agricultural land in the South."[6] The "black belt," a swath of fertile, generally dark soil extending from South Carolina through central Georgia and central Alabama, across north-central Mississippi, and farther west into parts of Arkansas, Louisiana, and eastern Texas, constituted the heart of plantation agriculture.[7] Lying in level or rolling tracts, Brannen concluded "plantation lands are practically always naturally fertile or capable of being made highly productive by the use of commercial fertilizers and manures or by crop rotation."[8]

The 270 plantation counties under consideration here contained a population of 7,195,600 in 1910. Substantially in excess of 50 percent of this population—3,933,627—was black, which was 40 percent of the black population of the United States in that census year. By contrast the 298 nonplantation counties contained a population of 6,288,076 in 1910, slightly less than 30 percent of which was black.

That the role played by the black population varied in the two groups of counties is suggested in Table 7, where information is provided on the distribution of black farms by tenure. There it is indicated that while only about 13 percent of the black farms in the plantation counties were owner cultivated, almost 40 percent of black farms in the nonplantation group were black owned. This evidence is generally supportive of the view that black farmers found it much

Table 7 Distribution of Black Farms by Tenure Status and County Type, 1910 (in percentages)

Tenure status	Plantation	Nonplantation
Owners, part owners, owners and tenants, managers	13.3	39.2
Cash tenants	48.4	25.1
Share tenants	38.3	35.7

Source: U.S. Bureau of the Census, *Census of the United States, 1900* (Washington, D.C.: GPO, 1902), vol. 5.

Table 8 Cotton's Share of the Value of Agricultural Production by County Type, 1880–1910 (in percentages)

Year	Plantation	Nonplantation
1880	71.3	42.6
1890	80.2	46.3
1900	51.6	24.1
1910	55.7	34.5

Source: U.S. Bureau of the Census, *Census of the United States, 1880* (Washington, D.C.: GPO, 1883), vol. 3; *Census of the United States, 1890* (Washington, D.C.: GPO, 1895), vol. 5; *Census of the United States, 1900* (Washington, D.C.: GPO, 1902), vol. 5; *Census of the United States, 1910* (Washington, D.C.: GPO, 1913), vol. 5.

more difficult to achieve an independent status in those areas of the South dominated by plantations than elsewhere in the region.

The plantation counties also differed from nonplantation counties in the extent to which their agricultural sector specialized in the production of cotton. As indicated in Table 8, between 1880 and 1910 cotton represented at least half the value of the agricultural output in the plantation counties, representing in excess of 70 percent in both 1880 and 1890. By contrast at no time did cotton in the nonplantation counties account for as much as half the value of agricultural production—the lowest level was 24 percent in 1900.

In general, then, one group of counties differed from the other not only with regard to the presence or absence of the plantation form of agricultural production, but also in the concentration of blacks in the population, the role played by blacks in agriculture, and the extent to which the agricultural sector specialized in cotton cultivation. Where plantation agriculture was concentrated, blacks found it most difficult to gain access to the ownership of land, which was typically employed in the production of the South's traditional staple. Charles S. Johnson summarized the situation as follows: present in the counties dominated by plantation agriculture was "a large untrained, Negro laboring force, few industrial or non farm occupations, low per capita incomes, a great gulf between the white-owning and white tenant population and between the white and Negro population, and rigid enforcement of racial restrictions."[9]

As we have seen, sharecropping and share tenancy became the organizational form of plantation agriculture because although the former slaves had successfully resisted the reimposition of gang labor, they had not been able to become landowners in large numbers. A similar tension continued throughout the period until World War I and even beyond. Writing in 1924 Brannen noted that planters would prefer to hire wage labor rather than employ tenants ". . . provided the supply could be relied upon." He reported that managerial flexibility was impaired because tenants, having invested in fertilizer and perhaps equipment, possessed a strong "interest in a particular tract of land." The result was "under the wage system, diversification, fertilizing, soil building and general upkeep are made easier and more economical." But it was also the case that wage workers typically were insufficiently available to allow wage-paying plantations to be viable. According to Brannen, "the supply of wage labor has been so uncertain and that which was available has been so unstable and unsatisfactory, that in many localities of the Cotton Belt little or no wage labor is employed other than the extra wage labor performed by the cropper and tenant families on the plantation."[10] Warren C. Whatley agrees with this assessment, arguing that "share tenancy helped a landlord secure much of the harvest labor at the beginning of the season and allowed him to circumvent some of the cost of depending on an uncertain and underdeveloped market for daily harvest labor."[11] Thus it is apparent that the sources of the tension which gave rise to the tenant plantation in the aftermath of the Civil War persisted fifty years later. The black agricultural labor force sought as much autonomy as possible, while the planters were interested in obtaining a reliable supply of closely supervised laborers. In light of the difficulty the black labor force encountered in its efforts to achieve the status

Table 9   Cultivated Plantation Acreage by Tenant Class, 1920

Tenant class	Acreage	% of Total
Croppers	2,601,735	33.3
Share tenants	2,749,282	35.2
Share cash	130,421	1.7
Standing	719,926	9.2
Cash	1,617,225	20.6
Total	7,818,589	100.0

Source: Calculated from C. O. Brannen, *Relation of Land Tenure to Plantation Organization*, U.S. Department of Agriculture, Department Bulletin, no. 1269, October 18, 1924, appendix C.

of landowner, sharecropping and various other forms of tenantry persisted as the organizational structure of plantation agriculture.

Sharecroppers and tenants were far more important sources of labor on the South's plantations than wage workers. In 1909, 71.5 percent of plantation land was operated by tenants and croppers, and in a sample of 207 plantations in 1920 this figure was 75.4 percent for all plantations and 81.3 percent for cotton plantations.[12] The relative importance of croppers on one hand and other tenantry forms on the other is not possible to assess before 1920 when the U.S. Department of Agriculture undertook a special investigation of the subject. The data collected in this 93-county study are brought together in Table 9. In this table a cropper is a farmer who contributes little to production except his/her labor and pays a share of the output as rental, while a share tenant pays his/her rent in the same way but does contribute equipment and work animals to production. In contrast to sharecropping and share tenancy, both standing renters and cash renters pay rentals which are fixed in advance, in the first case as a fixed amount of the output and in the second calculated on the basis of, typically, farm acreage. While share tenantry was slightly more important than sharecropping in terms of the proportion of plantation land under cultivation, the most significant fact emerging from Table 9 is that between them the two forms of tenancy which embodied rental as a share of output as opposed to a fixed rental accounted for 68.5 percent of the plantation land under cultivation. In practice a combination of tenantry forms was characteristic of plantation administration. As the USDA study reports "it happens, however, in the employment of labor on the plantation, that practically all imaginable combinations between pure wage agreements on the one hand and tenant contracts on the other, are to be found."[13] In fact similarities in the functioning of these tenantry systems, particularly those between sharecropping and share renting, were more important than their differences in the plantation South. A summary of field studies in the 1930s indicated that "the difference between these two classes is simply one of degree."[14] While a cropper contributed nothing to production besides labor, a share renter provided work animals and equipment. Nonetheless in both cases compensation was in the form of the "long pay," computed as a percentage of output at the harvest. This necessitated the extension of planter credit and required plantation workers to share in the risk associated with the cultivation of the crop.

However the most important similarity in all tenantry forms was planter supervision. Donald Alexander cites a cropper as saying that "when you work on a white man's place, you have to do what he says or treat, trade or travel." Planters were convinced that "the [plantation] laborer must be advised in practically all the details of his work, and be carefully watched in order to protect team, tools and crop which belong to the plantation owner."[15] It was this managerial function that was responsible for the fact that sharecroppers and tenants were not really independent farmers. As a result tenants typically did not have the opportunity to innovate in production methods on their own nor to gain managerial skills and experience.

This supervision, according to Brannen, "is nearly always understood in advance, which in cotton and tobacco sections, often amounts to the control of the cropper's or tenant's crop and the direction of the worker's farming activities by the landlord or manager." He goes on, "supervision is not the basis for distinguishing the cropper from the tenant. While croppers as a class are closely supervised, yet the difference in this respect is of little consequence on the plantation." Brannen reports that in a USDA survey of 215 plantations, 68 percent reported close supervision, 30 percent general supervision, and only 2 percent no supervision. Even more revealing, close supervision was reported on 81 percent of the 102 plantations using sharecroppers and 68 percent of those employing share renters.[16]

On a closely supervised tenant plantation every morning started with the ringing of a bell—referred to by Brannen as "one of the relics of the old regime."[17] Another bell, usually at sunrise, indicated the beginning of the work day and a bell at about sunset indicated the end of the day's labor. In this regard Brannen wrote that "the worker who fails to respond promptly to the bell, or the one who leaves the field before the bell sounds is questioned and unless a reasonable excuse is given he is usually reprimanded."[18]

Indeed it was the nature of the planter supervision which made that form of farm organization unique. As Morton Rubin put it in a post–World War II anthropological study, plantations were a "total sociocultural system." Within this system, Rubin writes, "the power structure of the plantation is authoritarian," in which a class/caste system results in a hierarchy running from a white owner at the top through white and black supervisors and taskmasters to black tenants at the bottom. He goes on to argue that the power and authority of the planter "enable him to control the human factor in the situation to a degree far exceeding comparable institutions in a supposedly democratic society." This results ultimately in the fact that "the plantation remains a last vestige of beneficent despotism."[19]

The ubiquity of the planters' control over the lives of estate residents clearly exceeded that of industrial managerial prerogatives over a firm's labor force. Residence on the plantation meant that the range of behavior over which planters could claim authority was exceedingly wide. Schooling, housing, and religion, as well as credit extension, are areas of worker activity which under capitalist industrial relations are not normally subject to direct managerial control, but under plantation conditions were subject to such authority. In Edgar Thompson's words, when the plantation worker "steals, fights, assembles, 'unlawfully' plots, marries secretly, indulges in fornication, has illegitimate children, spends his time in gambling, cockfighting or courting, the planter suffers some loss or threat of loss." As a result "the rise of rules and regulations and punishments for their violation have reference to all these things."[20]

In addition to the supervisory system a second distinctive feature of plantation agriculture was the system by which credit was extended to tenants. Because of the lien attached to their crops, share tenants and croppers normally had no access to primary sources of credit. They thus were forced to secure advances from their own landlords, a pattern referred to by Ransom and Sutch as a "territorial monopoly."[21] The latter was typically extended in two forms: cash advances and the provision of merchandise from a plantation store. Repayment of the loan occurred at the time the crop was sold. According to a 1926 survey of plantations in North Carolina, 82 percent of croppers received cash advances from planters; the average interest charge on these advances was 21 percent. In addition 60 percent of the croppers received household supplies through the extension of credit; the interest charge on these goods was 53 percent. Where plantation stores were not present tenants gained access to household supplies from merchants on the landlord's guarantee; this was the most expensive form of credit, with an average annual interest charge of 71 percent.[22] Comparable interest rates were found by Ransom and Sutch in their study of Georgia merchants, leading these authors to conclude that the rates charged "must be judged enormous when compared with credit charges at other times and other places in American history." Using the most generous estimate concerning supervisory costs and the risks of default, Ransom and Sutch conclude that no more than a 22.4 percent interest rate could have been obtained under competitive market conditions. Through much of the postbellum period such a rate was only about one-third the rate which actually prevailed in the South for blacks.[23]

Perhaps just as significant as the usurious levels at which interest rates stood were the limits on the ways credit could be used by plantation tenants. Credit can be a means to economic advance. When available at relatively low rates and employed for the purchase of investment goods, the extension of credit allows for the securing of resources which permit economic expansion. But in the plantation context credit availability for tenants was confined to retail purchases. As a result it was of little assistance to those attempting to mobilize resources for investment purposes.

Above and beyond these quantitative limitations problems also arose from the fact that in the planter-tenant relationship all accounts were kept by the planter. As a result the latter were under a constant temptation to manipulate records to their own benefit. Although the extent of cheating is impossible to document, one suspects that the amount of money involved was not trivial. A well-known story, although probably apocryphal, speaks to this issue. A tenant offering five bales of cotton was told, after some owl-eyed figuring, that his cotton exactly balanced his debt. Delighted at the prospect of a profit the tenant reported that he had one more bale which he hadn't brought in. "Shucks," shouted the boss, "why didn't you tell me before? Now I'll have to figure the account all over again to make it come out even.''[24]

Poverty was the condition which confronted virtually all black plantation tenants; as illustrated by Gilbert Fite's calculations, with the typical tenant farm between 15 and 30 acres, prevailing yields per acre and prices per pound could have resulted in nothing else. Thus, for example, in 1878 yields per acre under cotton came to about 148 pounds and prices averaged around $.08 to $.09 per pound. Gross revenue per acre, then, would come to $13.32 ($.09 × 148 pounds) resulting in revenue generated by each tenant farm averaging about $266. Of this, of course, only one-half belonged to the tenant, with the remaining half assigned to the planter. Furthermore, deductions from the tenant share were required for the cost of marketing the crop as well as for offsetting the credit plus interest which had been extended during the crop year. Fite notes that in such a circumstance it might well be the case that a cropper would receive no money at all at the end of the crop year.[25]

Black southern poverty thus was structural, an inherent aspect of the plantation organization of agriculture. Because cultivation occurred on lots which were too small with yields too low, the high rents and cost of interest could only result in poverty for plantation tenants. As Fite has put it the plantation tenants' "main problem . . . was lack of enough output to produce an adequate income for a decent living, to pay debts, or to accumulate any capital."[26] Black poverty, in short, was rooted in the organization and productivity of southern plantation agriculture.

The Limited Economic Development of the Plantation South

4

Fundamental to alleviating poverty is the process of economic development. There is little prospect of achieving rising standards of living broadly among a population unless the economy as a whole experiences what Simon Kuznets calls "modern economic growth." Advancing incomes occur when an economy's productivity increases and its structure of output widens. Thus an investigation of the persistence of black poverty requires an assessment of the South's postbellum experience with the process of modern economic growth, and the extent to which the plantation form of agriculture acts as an impediment to economic development.[1]

However, because the South was divided into plantation and nonplantation areas, analyses of regional development which do not take this division into account tend to produce misleading results. A case in point are evaluations made of the South's nineteenth-century economic development on the basis of per capita income estimates. The problem is that the subregional categories typically employed in grouping these data do not correspond to the differences between plantation and nonplantation areas. As a result growth rates reported for subregions mask differences within them.

The income estimates most frequently cited in this regard are provided in Table 10. These estimates seem to suggest that in all three subregions, the South's per capita income declined dramatically between 1840 and 1880. Thereafter the South's relative income tended to hold its own, indicating that the region's growth rate approximated that of the rest of the nation. These data thus are often viewed as support for the position that the South's postbellum economic institutions were growth promoting. In this interpretation the South experienced a devastating loss in wealth in the aftermath of the Civil War, but when that decline came to an end the South resumed growth at rates comparable to the rest of the rapidly developing country.[2]

However, because the Census Bureau classifications employed in these estimates do not correspond to the borders between the South's plantation and nonplantation regions, a question arises concerning the validity of this interpretation. Grouped on the census ba-

Table 10   Ratio of Regional Per Capita Income to National Per Capita Income, 1840–1920

	South Atlantic	East South Central	West South Central
1840	70	73	144
1880	45	51	60
1900	45	49	61
1920	59	52	72

Source: U.S. Bureau of the Census, *Historical Statistics of the United States, Colonial Times to 1970*, Bicentennial Edition, Part 1, Series F287–296 (Washington, D.C.: GPO, 1975).

sis it is not possible to determine whether plantation areas lagged in economic development. These data therefore do not cast light on the issue of whether the plantation system of agriculture retarded the process of modern economic growth. To do so the South has to be disaggregated so that the regions where plantation sharecropping was important are separated from the parts of the South where it was not. To the extent possible data are grouped according to these categories in Table 11.[3]

From this information it is clear that differences in economic growth did exist in the South and it was in its plantation areas that southern economic growth lagged the most. The percentage increase in per capita income for the nonplantation southern states between 1880 and 1900 was more than five times that of the plantation states. As a result the plantation states' per capita income by 1900 was 17 percent below that of the nonplantation southern states. Indeed nonplantation southern growth exceeded the 18.9 percent recorded for the nation as a whole. Thus there is no doubt that the aggregate growth data typically employed to describe southern economic expansion does hide the differential experience recorded in the plantation compared to the nonplantation south.

Because productivity growth is critical to long-term economic development, the relationship between plantation sharecropping and advancing technology is of importance in assessing the impact of the presence of a plantation economy on development. Available data allow a direct comparison of labor productivity in the South's plantation economy with that in agriculture elsewhere in the region. This comparison is provided in Table 12. Again the pattern is clear. Plantation

Table 11 Total Per Capita Income by State, 1880–1900 (in dollars)

| | Total Per Capita Income | | |
	1880	1900	Change (%)
Plantation states			
Alabama	56	62	10.7
Arkansas	62	63	1.6
Georgia	56	56	0.0
Louisiana	69	73	5.8
Mississippi	64	62	−3.1
South Carolina	51	57	11.8
Weighted mean*	59	62	5.1
Nonplantation states			
Florida	48	67	39.6
Kentucky	58	69	19.0
North Carolina	46	54	17.4
Tennessee	52	61	17.3
Texas	60	84	40.0
Virginia	51	66	29.4
West Virginia	54	79	46.3
Weighted mean*	53	69	30.2

Source: Richard A. Easterlin, "Interregional Differences in Per Capita Income, Population, and Total Income, 1840–1950," in *Trends in the American Economy—The Nineteenth Century*, vol. 24, Studies in Income and Wealth (Princeton: Princeton University Press, 1960), appendix A.
*Weighted by 1900 population.

agriculture is associated with a relatively poor productivity performance. Between 1880 and 1900 labor productivity in the southern states dominated by plantation agriculture declined 13.8 percent, while at the same time that measure increased 7.5 percent in the nonplantation South and more than 50 percent in agriculture for the United States as a whole.

Cotton dominated the plantation South. Insight into the productivity experience in cotton therefore is essential in understanding the plantation South's long-term pattern of development. Fortunately information compiled by the U.S. Department of Agriculture permits a comparison of productivity growth in cotton with that of other agricultural staples cultivated in nonplantation circumstances. This information is in the form of estimates of the man-hour re-

Table 12   Agricultural Income per Worker by State, 1880–1900 (in dollars)

	1880	1900	Change (%)
Plantation states			
Alabama	139	120	−13.7
Arkansas	197	147	−25.4
Georgia	145	134	−7.6
Louisiana	175	162	−7.4
Mississippi	180	142	−21.1
South Carolina	130	122	−6.2
Weighted mean*	159	137	−13.8
Nonplantation states			
Florida	115	140	21.7
Kentucky	173	174	0.6
North Carolina	139	130	−6.5
Tennessee	178	146	−18.0
Texas	167	228	36.5
Virginia	152	172	13.2
West Virginia	158	162	2.5
Weighted mean*	161	173	7.5
United States	252	386	53.2

Source: See table 10.
*Weighted by 1900 population.

quirements necessary to produce a 500-pound bale of cotton and 100 bushels of wheat and corn over a period dating from 1840 to 1920. A decrease in these measures indicates an increase in labor productivity and stands as a proxy for technological change. By comparing the performance of cotton on one hand and wheat and corn on the other, we are able to provide an initial test of the hypothesis that plantation agriculture inhibited the process of technological change. As indicated in Table 13 over the entire period the advance in labor productivity in cotton was less than half that in wheat and only about 60 percent of that in corn.

These results, however, are themselves a function of changes in two other variables—man-hour requirements per acre and yields per acre. A decrease in man-hour requirements per acre, assuming yields to be constant, would show up as a decrease in man-hours per unit

Table 13   Percentage Change in Man-Hour Levels for Wheat, Corn, and Cotton Production, 1840–1920

Years	Wheat	Corn	Cotton
1840–80	− 34.8	− 34.8	− 30.8
1880–1900	− 28.9	− 18.3	− 6.9
1900–20	− 19.4	− 23.1	− 0.6
1840–1920	− 62.7	− 59.1	− 36.0

Source: Calculated from Martin R. Cooper, Glen T. Barton and Albert P. Brodell, *Progress of Farm Mechanization*, U.S. Department of Agriculture, Miscellaneous Publications no. 630 (Washington, D.C.: GPO, 1947), table 1.
Note: Data are based on 100 bushels of wheat and corn and 500 pound bales of cotton.

Table 14   Percentage Change in Man-Hour per Acre Levels for Wheat, Corn, and Cotton Production, 1840–1920

Years	Wheat	Corn	Cotton
1840–80	− 42.9	− 33.3	− 11.9
1880–1900	− 25.0	− 17.4	− 5.9
1900–20	− 20.0	− 15.8	− 19.6
1840–1920	− 65.7	− 53.6	− 33.3

Source: See Table 10.

of output. The same would be the case were there an increase in yields, holding man-hour per acre requirements constant. Thus movements in labor productivity are determined by movements in land productivity or yields, and in man-hour requirements per acre— a proxy for farm mechanization. Changes in these two variables are reported in Tables 14 and 15, while the contribution of each separately to the overall increase in labor productivity is reported in Table 16.

The principal conclusions that emerge from Tables 13 through 16 are described in the following.

First, the rate of labor productivity advance during the period 1840–1920 was slower for cotton than the other two commodities. Cotton's slow growth was particularly marked in the period 1900–1920 (Table 13).

Second, the principal determinant of the rate of productivity advance for all three crops was mechanization. In only one instance did

Table 15   Percentage Change in Wheat, Corn, and Cotton Production Levels per Acre, 1840–1920

Years	Wheat	Corn	Cotton
1840–80	−12.0	2.4	27.3
1880–1900	5.3	1.2	0.1
1900–20	0.1	9.7	−19.2
1840–1920	−8.0	13.6	3.8

Source: See Table 10.
Note: Wheat and corn production based on bushels per acre; cotton production based on gross cotton lint per acre.

Table 16   Percentage Effect of Mechanization on Man-Hour Level Decreases for Wheat, Corn, and Cotton Production, 1840–1920

Years	Wheat	Corn	Cotton
1840–80	124.7	95.8	38.5
1880–1900	86.4	95.7	90.5
1900–20	102.0	70.6	285.0
1840–1920	105.3	90.8	92.7

Source: See Table 10.
Note: Data are based on 100 bushels for corn and wheat and 500 pound-bales of cotton. Figures are calculated by assuming that yields remained constant over the relevant years, but using actual decrease in man-hour requirements per acre for these same years and calculating percentage of total decrease in man-hour requirements per unit of output contributed by the latter.

the movement in yields (Table 15) outweigh the movement associated with mechanization in influencing changes in labor productivity (Table 14). Thus the slow growth in labor productivity in cotton can be attributed to the slow process of mechanization in this crop relative to the others.

Third, the sharp advance in labor productivity in cotton between 1840 and 1880 was the one instance in which changes in yields outweighed change in mechanization (Tables 14 and 15). In this case it is probable that increasing yields are associated with the westward movement of the locus of cotton cultivation. On the other hand the period in which mechanization proceeded most rapidly in cotton, 1900–20 (Table 14), did not see a substantial rise in labor productivity because during these years yields in cotton declined sharply—probably because of the boll weevil infestation (Table 15).

The period 1840–1920 was therefore one in which cotton lagged behind the other crops in labor productivity and mechanization.[4] By the end of the period the process of mechanization had accelerated, which failed to show up in increased labor productivity only because of an exogenous factor affecting yields.

One possible explanation of the lag in productivity growth in cotton relative to other crops might simply be because the engineering problems involved in designing a cotton picker were more difficult than the technology required for other crops. James H. Street lists several factors which made it difficult to mechanize the cotton harvest. First was that soil types varied and machinery suited to some circumstances was unworkable in others. Differences in the genetic characteristics of the cotton plant and variations in cultivation practices also made the adoption of a mass-produced harvester difficult. These differences, however, appear to be unlikely sources of a long-term lag in technology; Street notes that such problems might have affected a mass-marketed harvester but still would have permitted the development of several machines, each suited to local conditions.[5] A more serious problem was that bolls on the cotton plant do not ripen at a uniform rate, which necessitates a harvester that strips the plant of the ripened bolls but leaves intact and uninjured the unripened bolls. With handpicking this problem requires that pickers go over the same plant three or four times. A similar process was required of a mechanical picker.

Notwithstanding this problem Street argues that these technical difficulties were not the principal reasons that technology lagged in cotton.[6] Indeed Heywood Fleisig has discovered that advanced harvesting techniques were available in the years between the end of the Civil War and World War I but were simply not adopted. Thus he writes of an Arkansas planter threshing his cotton in the 1860s, a Texas farmer reporting in the 1890s of successfully using a Cunningham cotton picker, and the appearance of a "sled" for harvesting at the time of World War I, a piece of equipment Fleisig describes as "well within the reach of nineteenth century technology."[7] Furthermore Gilbert Fite reports that although improved equipment such as cottonseed planters, fertilizer spreaders, stalk cutters, and improved plows and harrows became available, they largely went unutilized:

Table 17   Average Annual Number of Patents Granted for Wheat, Corn, and Cotton Production, 1837/59–1900/19

Years	Wheat	Corn	Cotton
1837–59	10.3	12.4	1.2
1860–79	35.4	34.2	11.1
1880–99	57.2	48.7	25.9
1900–1919	47.1	63.0	46.1
1837–1919	35.9	37.8	20.5

Source: Jacob Schmookler, "Time Series of Patents Classified by Industry, United States, 1837–1957," in Zvi Griliches and Leonid Hurwicz (eds.), *Patents, Inventions, and Economic Change: Data and Selected Essays* (Cambridge: Harvard University Press, 1972), pp. 100–103.

Note: Figures for wheat and corn production include patents for harvesting, threshing, and cutting; figures for cotton production include patents for harvesting, picking, and chopping plows.

"[e]xcept for plowing which was done with mule and horse power, cotton growing was mainly a hand operation."[8]

In this connection Jacob Schmookler's data on patents issued by crop and process also seem to support Street's skepticism. For what the patent data indicate are efforts to find technological solutions, not the commercial viability of those solutions themselves. As is clear in Table 17 throughout the nineteenth century at least, far more patents were issued related to grain and corn cultivation than cotton. Seen from this perspective cotton is significant because so few efforts were made to solve the technical problems, not that the technical problems remained unsolved at a relatively late date.

This limited effort was the key to the delay in achieving a mechanical breakthrough in cotton. The difficulty encountered in cotton harvesting was simply the mechanical problem of not injuring the cotton plant while stripping it of the fiber, as opposed to the application of new scientific principles. Furthermore the basic problem of leaving undamaged unripened cotton bolls was not different from that faced in corn where there was a need to separate the ear from the stalk while preserving the stalk for forage.[9] It thus appears unlikely that the level of theoretical science and technology adequately account for the lag in technological advance in cotton. Overall the evidence in-

Table 18   Change in Production Levels and Prices of Wheat, Corn, and Cotton, 1881/85–1906/10 (in percentages)

	Wheat	Corn	Cotton
Production level	40.1	58.0	95.1
Price	0.6	21.6	17.1

Source: U.S. Bureau of the Census, *Historical Statistics of the United States, Colonial Times to 1957,* Series K265-273 and K298-306 (Washington, D.C.: GPO, 1960).

dicates that at least during the nineteenth century, mechanization and inventive activity proceeded at a slower pace in cotton than in other agricultural staples.

Schmookler attempted to account for variations in inventive activity by pointing to the incentive to engage in this kind of behavior. He theorized that the sale of capital goods to an industry would be associated with the demand for that industry's output in the product market. In turn the expected gain from inventive activity "varies with the expected sale of improved capital goods embodying the inventions and [that] expected sale of improved capital goods are largely determined by present capital goods sales."[10] Thus the stronger the demand for the product the higher the level of capital goods sales to the industry producing the product, and, because of this, the greater the anticipated potential returns from inventive activity. Thus the incentive to engage in inventive activity in the production of equipment for a particular industry is positively associated with the demand for the final goods produced by that industry.

Schmookler's demand hypothesis would find confirmation where a relatively slow growth in productivity is associated with a weak market performance. Such an experience might lead to lower levels of investment and, because of that, a reduced incentive to engage in inventive activity. This in turn would show up in low rates of technological change. Thus a fairly simple test of the Schmookler hypothesis with regard to the lag in productivity growth in cotton would be to compare the cotton market with the market for the other two crops considered in this chapter—wheat and corn.

In Table 18 we compare the price and output experience of wheat, corn, and cotton between 1881–85 and 1906–10. These years were selected so as to avoid those immediately after the Civil War, which would have shown an even larger increase in market prices than appears in this table. But to do so would have been to exaggerate the strength of the cotton market since for much of this period southern cotton was merely reestablishing its position in the market and not responding to new market opportunities.

Line 1 in Table 18 shows that over the period the production of cotton grew more rapidly than was the case for corn or wheat. But line 2 indicates that while this was occurring the price of cotton rose, an increase comparable to that of corn and superior to that of wheat— which held about constant. Increases in price occurring at the same time output is advancing suggest that the demand for the product was increasing even more than the supply. These data thus suggest that the market for cotton was stronger than for either of the two other crops. That cotton output increased much more than corn while their price trends were similar suggests a more favorable shift in demand for cotton than corn. Similarly the superior experience of cotton in both product and price indicates the presence of a stronger market for cotton than for wheat.

That the cotton market was stronger than the market for corn or wheat is inconsistent with Schmookler's hypothesis. Cotton experienced a lower level of productivity growth than the other two crops, but unlike what would be anticipated following Schmookler's line of reasoning this relatively poor performance in productivity was not associated with a weaker product market.

Thus an explanation of the technological retardation in the plantation cultivation of cotton must locate the relative disincentive to engage in productivity-raising behavior in the internal organization of cotton agriculture rather than its product market. A thesis consistent with this requirement has been advanced by Warren C. Whatley. According to Whatley it was critical that tenants were retained under contract until the end of the crop year. The problem was that under such an arrangement the introduction of an advanced technique would not reduce labor costs at all if it did not allow the planter to contract with fewer workers for the entire crop year. But such a reduction could be accomplished only if the new technology raised productivity in all phases of production in which intense labor demand was present. As a result there was little payoff to incremental technological advance. In this connection Whatley cites the observation of researchers and field agents of the Department of Agriculture as arguing that "the maintenance of a labor force to meet these peak needs has not provided inducement for the widespread adoption of labor-saving machinery when labor is employed on a share basis." Commenting on this Whatley argues that it was not the share feature of the contract which caused the problem. Rather the bottleneck derived from the "long-term nature of the contract and the fact that the payment to labor was not tied directly to the number of hours worked."[11]

It was this disincentive to achieve continuous piecemeal technical advances which seems most dramatically to differentiate southern plantation agriculture from that of the rest of the country. Independent proprietors constituted the bulk of agriculturalists in the North and the Midwest. Motivated by the fact that any advance in productivity would result either in increased income or reduced costs, these farmers continuously experimented with new crops and cultivation techniques in an effort to improve their profitability. Parker writes that northern farms "were amateur research laboratories and technical schools as well as production organizations . . . [which] could out-compete any appreciably larger-scale organization of a labor force, and did so rather decisively when put to the test."[12] No such rewards for incremental effort appeared in the plantation context. As a result the continuous process of innovation characteristic of the family farm system of the North was not present in the plantation context of the South.

Although Whatley does not use the concept of the plantation economy, his thesis concerning the lag in technological advance in cotton is consistent with it. For obviously there was more behind the use of the long-term contract than the seasonal demand for labor. If land had been made available to the former slaves a family farm system would have been created and landless agricultural workers on a large scale would not have been available to southern planters. Under such circumstances the question of a long-term contract would not have arisen as the southern agricultural structure would have resembled the owner-occupier system of the rest of the country. Thus the source of the technological retardation of the South's agriculture resides in the history of the region and the means by which plantation agriculture was able to survive the ending of slavery.

The poorly developed educational system of the plantation South reinforced the bias against technological progress. In Table 19 I present two indices of education: the illiteracy rate and the percentage of the school-age population attending classes. Changes in

Table 19   Illiteracy and School Attendance by State, 1860–1900 (in percentages)

	1860		1880		1900	
	Illiteracy[a]	School Attendance[b]	Illiteracy	School Attendance[b]	Illiteracy	School Attendance[b]
Plantation states						
Alabama	23.7	25.3	29.3	39.4	21.1	32.8
Arkansas	16.5	24.0	19.1	36.2	11.6	43.5
Georgia	22.7	31.4	39.0	41.1	18.9	35.4
Louisiana	27.4	20.1	31.6	24.1	35.9	28.6
Mississippi	33.6	20.6	27.9	54.8	19.8	40.9
South Carolina	34.3	16.9	32.3	36.4	22.3	68.1
Weighted mean[c]	26.4	25.0	28.5	38.4	20.0	40.4
Nonplantation states						
Florida	23.4	15.4	26.1	43.5	13.8	44.0
Kentucky	14.0	40.3	15.7	47.1	10.0	48.3
North Carolina	21.2	29.9	26.3	49.9	16.7	42.1
Tennessee	16.6	36.7	19.1	50.0	12.2	43.7
Texas	14.0	27.3	16.1	30.1	9.0	42.4
Virginia	19.0	25.4	23.8	40.0	14.8	42.8
West Virginia	—	—	8.4	61.7	6.1	52.3
Weighted mean[c]	17.3	31.9	19.6	45.1	11.7	44.5

Sources: U.S. Bureau of the Census, *Census of the United States* [for each year], vol. 1: *Population* (Washington, D.C.: GPO).
[a]Slaves over 20 in 1860 are assumed to be illiterate and not attending school.
[b]School age is 5–19 inclusive in 1860 and 1880 and 5–20 in 1900.
[c]Weighted by population at each census year.

census definitions may tend to impair the comparability of these data over time. Nonetheless the pattern is clear. Measured in either way educational achievement in the plantation South lagged behind the rest of the South, not to mention the North. As late as 1900 the illiteracy rate stood at 20 percent in the plantation states compared to 11.7 percent in the other southern states, while school attendance rates also were inferior in the plantation states throughout the period.

These data suggest that the people of the plantation South were generally less well equipped to participate in and contribute to the technological dynamism associated with modern economic growth. Their relatively low levels of education meant that they were much less likely than people elsewhere in the United States to be the source of technological innovation. Furthermore that so many residents of the plantation economy were illiterate meant that their ability to employ relatively advanced cultivation techniques was constrained, particularly if such techniques required reading and understanding written instructions. Because its population was relatively deprived of education, the Deep South was less likely to be at the frontier of technological innovation than regions where the population was better educated.

The low level of educational attainment present in the plantation South seems likely to have been both a consequence and a cause of that system of agriculture. Because new techniques were not eagerly sought after in plantation cultivation, a well-educated population was not essential to the profitability of the economy. But at the same time that absence of well-trained and educated individuals tended to result in the perpetuation of the region's technical backwardness. All of this may help to explain why, in Wright's formulation, the South "lacked a strong indigenous technological tradition and a 'southern' technical community developing an advanced southern version of new innovations."[13]

The functioning of plantation agriculture thus tended to reduce the capability and the incentive to engage in technological change. So did the cost and relative unavailability of capital funds. Lance Davis has analyzed how in the evolution of the U.S. capital market between 1870 and 1914 "the South stood apart." Neither long- nor short-term markets effectively developed in the region. Interest rates in the South were considerably higher than elsewhere, with relatively few banks present. What accounted for the differential experience by region in the evolution of capital markets is not yet clear, with Davis remarking that "the question of why the South lagged is still open."[14]

What is clear is that the undeveloped capital market in the South also contributed to the slow pace of productivity growth there. Credit was both more expensive and less available than it would have been if the market in that region was as well developed as those elsewhere. The high price of financing provided a disincentive for capital investment; but to the extent that technological change is embodied in new machinery, it was precisely this disincentive that resulted in a lower rate of productivity growth than would have been the case if the cost of credit to finance investment had been lower.[15]

What all of this means is that cotton planters had both less incentive and less ability to search for and implement new methods of production than did farmers elsewhere in the United States. Incremental mechanization tended not to result in a reduction in labor costs and therefore was less sought after than was the case in parts of the country where agriculture was dominated by owner-occupiers. In addition credit, essential to the financing of technical innovation, was both more expensive and less available than elsewhere. Furthermore there was a lack of the kind of well-trained and educated individuals who could engage in the research necessary to sustain a long-term process of technical innovation. Plantation agriculture, in short, resulted in both a reduced incentive and capability to achieve the kind of technological progress characteristic of modern economic growth than did the family farm system of agriculture.

Racial discrimination in both the South and the North had to a considerable extent confined the African American labor force to southern plantation agriculture after the Civil War. Organized on a share tenant or sharecropping basis, plantation production, though profitable, resulted in a slower pace of technical innovation and labor productivity growth than occurred in agriculture elsewhere in the country. The reestablishment of the plantation system thus perpetuated the lag in economic modernization that originated during the period of slavery. Southern underdevelopment was rooted in the region's characteristic system of agriculture, which itself was dependent upon limited occupational choice by blacks. Black deprivation therefore was both a consequence and a cause of southern underdevelopment, which in turn resulted in the continuation of poverty among African Americans.

The Plantation Economy

5

The authoritarianism of plantation life found a counterpart in the wider politics of the plantation South. Fundamental was the exclusion of southern blacks from electoral participation. A black politics had existed during Reconstruction: indeed Eric Foner writes that "rarely has a community invested so many hopes in politics as did Blacks during Radical Reconstruction"; based on black bloc voting, Republicans came into office through the South.[1] But gradually through the 1870s this high tide of political involvement was pushed back. When Rutherford B. Hayes was elected President in 1876, federal protection of black political participation in the South was removed. Quickly thereafter African American disenfranchisement became the regional rule.

The consequences of this exclusion from political life were manifested in two dimensions. First, it meant that the political hegemony long maintained in the South by the planters and their allies was permitted to continue.[2] Second, it meant that the specific interests of the share tenants and black population generally went virtually unrecognized in political decisionmaking. Thus Robert Higgs has emphasized how this exclusion biased public appropriations away from the African American population. With regard to education, for example, he writes that the result of this skewing was "ramshackle and poorly equipped school houses, incompetent teachers and half-taught pupils—and in many districts not even this much. . . ."[3] Hostile laws and selective law enforcement were the norm, largely because blacks had virtually no redress through the political process. In this way the long years of political exclusion resulted in a pattern of domination which reinforced a similar experience encountered within the confines of the plantations themselves.

Cut off from the North, subjected to economic privation, racial discrimination, authoritarian supervision, and without a political means to ameliorate their situation, African Americans in the South were entrapped in a milieu different from that experienced by any other group in the United States. To capture this context it is appropriate to describe it as a plantation economy. That phrase is intended both to convey the specific economic activity central to black life in the South and to underline the continuity which prevailed despite the undeniable importance of emancipation.

That the South in the postbellum period can best be characterized as a plantation economy can be traced to the work of Ulrich Phillips. Writing in 1910 Phillips argued that the plantation system "was less dependent upon slavery than slavery was upon it." According to Phillips the plantation system formed "the industrial and social frame of government in the black-belt communities." In this perspective slavery represented "a code of written laws enacted for the furtherance of that system's purposes." Emancipation required the plantation communities to "provide new laws and customs for the adjustment of employers and employees." After the Civil War the transition had been successfully completed in the black belt and the plantation system continued as "the most common tether" linking the black and white races.[4]

The thesis that a "plantation system" was present in the postbellum South was subsequently taken up by the sociologist Edgar T. Thompson. Thompson writes that "the Civil War did not, contrary to an opinion often encountered outside of the South, destroy the plantation system, [though] it did profoundly alter the legal status of one of its elements, labor."[5] Thompson argued that it was the South's plantation system which resulted in "a culture which was to differentiate it from other regions of the United States and perhaps of the world." According to Thompson the region's plantation system was the "institutional fault line" separating the South from the rest of the country." [W]hatever is 'different' whatever is special about the South," writes Thompson, "appears to go back to the plantation and to the system of institutions which have grown up around it."[6]

Thompson insists that a plantation should not be understood simply as a large farm which produces output for a market. It does do that, of course, but it is also "the economic and political base of an institutional hierarchy." In it "its chief of state, the planter, may exercise almost complete authority or acquire immunities from the laws of the larger state of which he became a part." Thompson writes that workers on plantations may be slaves, indentured servants, contract laborers, or sharecroppers, but whatever is the case "the hallmark of their condition is obedience whether induced by compulsion, custom, habit or even reverence." The mutual acceptance of myth typically is required to sustain such hierarchy and, writes Thompson, "in plantation societies generally this tends to take the form of a belief in inferior and superior races." What all of this results in is the emergence of a "distinctive 'way of life' common, up to a point, to all its members." In this there was "often exhibited in the relations between the races the extremes of kindness on the one hand and of brutal cruelty on the other, and sometimes a strange combination of both." This "customary ethic," according to Thompson "ordinarily . . . is not reflected upon; it is just expected as a matter of second nature." He goes on

> It does not involve the application of force, it is not a matter of conscience, but it has, nevertheless, a compelling quality. Those who have attacked the Southern "way of life" have not recognized its presence, and it is so far beneath the level of public consciousness that Southerners, even in their best writings and oratory, have not been able to give it adequate expression, although this is what Mark Twain tried to do in Huckleberry Finn.[7]

Those familiar with the work of Antonio Gramsci will at once recognize that what Thompson is describing is a manifestation of "cultural hegemony." As developed by Gramsci this concept refers to

> an order in which a certain way of life and thought is dominant, in which one concept of reality is diffused throughout society in all its institutional and private manifestations, informing with its spirit all taste, morality, customs, religious and political principles, and all social relations, particularly in their intellectual and moral connotations.[8]

Even under slavery, where force was a central element in the master-slave relationship, the use of violence did not typify everyday life. Although coercion was the ultimate sanction available to the slaveowners, social viability required that a pattern of mutual accommodation between slaves and slaveowners be formed. It is in this connection that Eugene D. Genovese has argued that "a paternalism accepted by both masters and slaves—but with radically different interpretations—afforded a fragile bridge across the intolerable contradictions inherent in a society based on racism, slavery and class exploitation that had to depend on the willing reproduction and productivity of its victims." The ideology of paternalism, writes Genovese, "defined the involuntary labor of the slaves as a legitimate return to their masters for protection and direction." Notwithstanding that "brutality lies inherent in this acceptance of patronage and dependence" and that it "may have reinforced racism as well as class exploitation," Southern paternalism nevertheless "recognized the slaves' humanity—not only their free will but the very talent and ability without which their acceptance of a doctrine of reciprocal obligations would have made no sense."[9]

Although he recognizes that paternalism persisted in the postbellum period, Genovese believes that "the destruction of slavery meant the end of paternalism as the reigning ideal of social relations." In the New South of labor markets the paternalism which remained was the result of the fact that "some planters and tenants have fought a rear-guard action against its erosion."[10] As illustrative of this change Genovese cites a Louisiana planter in a deposition filed with the Union army as reporting, "When I owned niggers, I used to pay medical bills. I do not think I shall trouble myself."[11] James Roark adopts a similar position. Although Roark concedes that "despite the magnitude of the pressures acting against paternalism, emancipation did not mark the end of feelings of genuine concern for one's laborers" and that "the aristocratic tradition did not die out with the old regime or even the old aristocrats,"[12] he nonetheless emphasizes that in the new labor contracts negotiated between tenants and croppers, planters often excluded responsibility for the costs of medical care, burial expenses, the cost of Sunday preachers, and rations for those who did not work. From this he concludes that "there was a noticeable abandonment of paternalism" in the postbellum period.[13] Michael Wayne adopts the same point of view in asserting that "when the freedmen took to the road and introduced the marketplace into the labor settlement, the old relations did not weaken; they crumbled."[14] Paternalism in this view is the product of slavery—that is, nonmarket-determined labor relations. With the presence of a labor market, paternalism becomes a cultural atavism.

In contrast Gunnar Myrdal as late as the 1940s wrote that paternalism was still strong. He believed "paternalism is cherished particularly as the ideal relation between whites and Negroes. The Southerner is proud of his benevolence toward Negro dependents but would resent vigorously their demanding this aid as a right." He goes on to argue that this paternalism ". . . is based on a clear and unchallenged recognition from both sides of an insurmountable social inequality."[15] Numerous commentators noted that the acceptance of deferential patterns of behavior was the necessary condition for southern blacks to achieve the status of landowner. Arthur P. Raper in his discussion of two black belt counties in the 1930s argued that the single-most important attribute of a successful black landowner was acceptability to the dominant community. Raper writes:

> Being acceptable here is no empty phrase. It means that he and his family are industrious and that his credit is good. It means that he is considered safe by local white people—he knows "his place" and stays in it. Though it varies somewhat from one community to another and from one individual to another, the definition of "his place" hedges the Negro landowner about by restrictions similar to those which define and enforce the chronic dependency of landless Negroes. . . ."[16]

Indeed the sale of land itself frequently was an act of patronage. W. T. Couch argues that "often the purchase will have been made at the suggestion of a white man who wishes to do a favor to a Negro whom he likes."[17] By being able to reward socially acceptable behavior in this way, the white community armed itself with positive rewards in addition to negative sanctions. At the same time seen from the perspective of the southern black population, the acceptance of such patronage, although costly in terms of a claim to an egalitarian way of life, nonetheless opened space for the achievement of black aspirations—in this case landownership.

Not all southern African Americans after the Civil War accommodated themselves to the demands of paternalism. The novelist Richard Wright, for example, reports that he found it impossible consistently to adopt the appropriately deferential manner. In his autobiography Wright recalls that in response to the entreaties of his friends he would attempt to adjust to the requirements of his circumstance—being black in the South. But try as he might he found it "utterly impossible . . . to calculate, to scheme, to act, to plot all the time." He recalls "I would remember to dissemble for short periods, then I would forget and act straight and human again, not with the desire to harm anybody, but merely forgetting the artificial status of race and class."[18] However, as Wright himself understood, this unwillingness or inability to accept the region's social etiquette was not typical. At stake were both negative and positive incentives. Violating the cultural norms of the region was to risk triggering the use of force, whereas positive incentives were present for the outward acceptance of a racial etiquette.

There is no dispute among commentators concerning the continued existence of paternalism in the postbellum South. Rather the

issue is whether paternalism represented the South's cultural hegemony after the emancipation as it had before the Civil War. Specifically the question is whether with the elimination of the master-slave
relationship a new form of paternalism, one specific to a plantation
economy where juridical freedom was present, had emerged. If the
paternalism of the antebellum period was a product of the nonmarket
relationship between planter and slave before the Civil War the question is whether a new paternalism was associated with the constrained
labor market which faced southern blacks in the antebellum period.

Recent theoretical work by Lee J. Alston and Joseph F. Ferrie
has argued precisely that paternalism is likely to emerge in a social
setting like that of the postbellum South. Alston and Ferrie define
paternalism as "a relationship involving employer provision of a wide
range of goods and services in exchange for loyal service and a measure of deference."[19] Subjected to the social and political dominance
of white planters, "workers—especially blacks—had an incentive to
entrust themselves to a protector who could provide the security and
the services the worker was unable to obtain for himself. . . ." At the
same time paternalism was attractive to the planters because it served
"to increase non supervised work intensity, limit worker mobility and
instill in workers a longer time horizon." Alston and Ferrie write that
"if landlords have access to the machinery of the state and can foster
a discriminatory environment . . . they are able to increase the value
of the paternalistic goods they supply."[20] Thus in a society in which
production required a steady application of mass labor and in which
the providers of that labor were subjected to racial discrimination,
paternalism emerged as functional to each side.

Paternalism, in short, is not simply a nonmarket phenomenon.
It may be present as part of the market relationship between the powerful and the nonpowerful, where the latter has little likelihood of
overcoming its relatively weak position and the former is intent on
trading on its dominance. In such a context the paternalistic provision
of compensation in the form of housing, garden plots, grazing rights,
firewood, wagon and mule use, hunting privileges, and credit may be
the result of the bargaining between unequals. According to Alston
the tenantry practiced in the South involving these ancillary forms
of compensation "increased the dependency of blacks on whites and
[in turn] this dependency created an economic incentive for upholding
traditional race etiquette." Of course to argue that this was the result
of market relations is not to imply that bargaining was between

equals. Rather, as Alston writes, "it means only that given the existing socioeconomic institutional framework, blacks had an economic incentive to adopt a subservient role."[21] Market paternalism thus is not a contradiction in terms.

The South's paternalism by no means precluded the use of violence. Although a relatively inefficient instrument by which to achieve social cohesion, the use of force was omnipresent as a backup means to ensure social viability. And, indeed, the use of terror was a part of the postbellum southern way of life. Thus the anthropologists Davis, Gardner, and Gardner in examining the administration of whippings found the following pattern:

> Periodically there seems to develop a situation in which a number of Negroes begin to rebel against the caste restrictions. This is not an open revolt but a gradual pressure, probably more or less unconscious, in which, little by little, they move out of the strict pattern of approved behavior. The whites feel this pressure and begin to express resentment. They say the Negroes are getting "uppity," that they are getting out of their place and that something should be done about it. . . . A Negro does something which ordinarily might be passed over, or which usually provokes only mild resentment, but the whites respond with violence. The Negro becomes both a scapegoat and an object lesson for his group. . . . After such an outburst, the Negroes again abide strictly by the caste rules, the enmity of the whites is dispelled and the tension relaxes. The whites always say after such an outburst, "We haven't had any trouble since then."[22]

Violence thus was employed in reaction to a violation of approved behavioral norms, particularly attempts to escape deferential patterns by southern blacks. Furthermore this use of violence was aimed not only at the individual transgressor, but also possessed symbolic importance for the other members of the black community. The ability to inflict violence on one individual acted as a deterrent against attempts to introduce more egalitarian behavioral patterns.

Data on the use of violence and force in the South in this period are very poor and difficult to interpret. Even if provided with data on the number of acts of violence committed in a year, it is hard to assess what proportion of all such acts a particular number represents, or how wide was the resulting circle of intimidation. The one act of violence for which fairly systematic data are available is for lynchings. In 1905 James Elbert Cutler estimated that there were 1,449 lynchings between 1882 and 1903 in the states of Alabama, Arkansas, Georgia,

Louisiana, Mississippi, and South Carolina. Of the victims, 83.7 percent were blacks. During these years, then, there was an average of 69 lynchings per annum in these states, a figure large enough to suggest that blacks knew that the threat of violence associated with nonconforming behavior was real.[23]

Precisely because of their subordinate status in society, and the reality that violence could be used against them, blacks had no choice but to accommodate to the protection associated with a patron-client relationship. Similarly because of the dominance they exercised and influence they wielded, planters were able to dispense the protections which their tenants sought. Thus it is that not only did the constraints experienced by black labor produce poverty, but confinement to the plantation economy was associated with a culture unique to the South. As Edgar T. Thompson has written:

> Separating the South from the other sections of the United States is an institutional fault line. The basic institutions—the school, the church, the family—are, of course, present in all sections, but in the South they are parts of the plantation 'system' as they are parts of other societal systems elsewhere. It is the plantation which is not continuous with other sections of America, and the institutions which are part of the plantation system are not, therefore, exactly continuous with similar institutions in other parts of America.[24]

The institution of the plantation thus shaped the dynamic of southern society and moved it in a direction profoundly at variance to that experienced in the rest of the country.

Cast in Marxist terms, that the trajectory of postbellum southern society was so decisively different from that of the rest of the country suggests it possessed a mode of production different from that present elsewhere. If for the rest of the United States a model of capitalism—a capitalist mode of production—provides useful insight into the pattern of economic growth and cultural change, a different model, that of a plantation economy, is necessary for the South.

A plantation economy is one in which the state of technology allows profit-maximizing, large-scale farmers to produce a staple primarily for an external market. That same technology, however, requires the use of more workers than would be made available if they were freely permitted to choose their employment in a competitive labor market. As a result a market imperfection—a limit on worker's ability to exercise choice—is required for planters to be sure of a sufficient supply of workers to carry out profitable production. Thus an impediment to labor mobility is necessary to a plantation economy, in contrast to capitalism where the operation of a free labor market is a dominant institutional feature of society.

The view that even after the Civil War a noncapitalist mode of production prevailed in the South has not, however, won wide acceptance among Marxists and has recently come under attack by two historians writing in that tradition. Barbara Jeanne Fields and Harold D. Woodman both reject the thesis that a distinctive noncapitalist mode of production persisted in the postbellum period, although they do accept Eugene D. Genovese's thesis that the antebellum slave South was different in character from the capitalist system present in the North before the Civil War. Fields writes that the "hybrid characteristics" of the southern economy after the Civil War "have led some people to the mistaken conclusion that nothing fundamental changed at all." In agreement Woodman argues that those who emphasize continuity "are not so much wrong as incomplete in their analysis. . . ."[25] Each historian recognizes that the system of labor relations which emerged during Reconstruction possessed elements of continuity with slavery. Nonetheless both Fields and Woodman believe that emancipation represented the introduction of capitalist relations in the region.

Fields allows that "it was certainly a peculiar brand of capitalism that slowly came to life in the South . . ." and Woodman acknowledges that "capitalism in the South differed from that in the North in a number of important ways that cannot be ignored. . . ." Neither believes that the shift from slavery to capitalism was rapid or abrupt. Fields writes that "after the epochmaking upheaval of the Civil War and Reconstruction, a prolonged period of transition set in. . . ." In a similar vein Woodman argues that the Civil War and Reconstruction "achieved only half a revolution; they destroyed an old economic system but created nothing to replace it. The establishment of a free labor economy and society had still to be completed."[26]

The problem is that neither Fields nor Woodman has constructed a model that comes to grips with the specificity of southern life. By describing the South as capitalist they give rise to the expectation of a society in which a free market in labor is a dominant institutional feature. In such a setting an individualism embodying universalistic and meritocratic principles would be expected. There,

too, following Marx, rapid economic change and technological transformation would be present.

As we have seen, however, neither a culture of individualistic
equality nor modern economic growth were salient in the postbellum South. Indeed subordination and paternalism typified relations
between white and black southerners, and technical stagnation characterized the production process in cotton. The source of these differentiating aspects of southern compared to northern life seems
clear. Still, in these years the black population had not achieved a
position from which to compete in markets on a basis of equality with
whites. Originating in the failure of land reform, circumstances dic-
tated that the largest concentration of black workers remained on cotton plantations after as well as before the Civil War, denied the
geographic, industrial, and occupation mobility experienced by other
subgroups in the U.S. population. Confined in this way to cotton
cultivation the black labor force was subjected to the unique cultural,
economic, and political deprivations associated with the plantation
way of life.

There is no *a priori* way to choose between the appropriateness
of two models of society. That choice depends on which better cap-
tures the salient elements of the society in question. In this case it
seems clear that the use of the capitalist mode of production to char-
acterize the South does not correspond adequately to the unique fea-
tures of that society. It therefore is not as useful as a plantation mode
of production—an analytic tool which emphasizes the sources of that
region's unique racial etiquette and economic underdevelopment in
characterizing the South.

Leaving the South

6

A plantation economy based on sharecropping instead of slavery was reconstituted in the South in the years following the Civil War. But the postbellum plantation economy was more fragile than the slavery system. Unlike the antebellum context, where the expression of employment preferences by slaves was a legal contradiction in terms, after the Civil War, choice among work options was no longer legally prohibited. Confinement to plantations was not juridically required. Instead the denial of work alternatives was circumstantial, dependent upon the limited resources possessed by African Americans and the racial animus possessed by northern and southern employers. In that sense the postbellum plantation structure was always more at risk than the system which preceded it. A change in the labor market outside of the plantation South could have had devastating consequences on that region.

Indeed interindustry and interregional immobility, although essential to the maintenance of the southern plantation economy, was profoundly at variance with the ideology and economic practice dominant in the rest of the country. Labor mobility—the movement of workers from relatively low productivity work to occupations where their productivity was higher—provided an important source of growth in the national economy.[1] Further the free market ideology dominant in the country approved and reinforced the view that labor should without interference be free to search out and secure jobs yielding higher rates of pay. Obviously, however, this dominant world view was in conflict with the racism which was practiced in the country. For while a free market ideology in principle is color-blind, the denial of employment to African Americans in the North and the denial of full legal and civil rights in the South was the dominant reality experienced by the black population.

At least until World War I the contradiction between free market ideology and the reality of racial discrimination was not costly to the North. The confinement of African Americans to the South did not retard growth because an alternative source of labor was available from Europe. Between 1870 and 1910 immigration to the United

States averaged about 500,000 per year, amounting to a very high migration rate of 7.6 migrants per 1,000 of the population per year. Under these circumstances there was little need for black labor outside of the South. The inflow of population to the United States meant that northern employers could hire migrants from Europe and indulge their racist prejudices at little or no cost in terms of their foregone production or profits.

World War I, however, marked the beginning of the end of African American confinement to the South and its plantation economy. Before the outbreak of hostilities the region's plantation system rested on a rather delicate equilibrium in which the "external" demand for labor had not overwhelmed the "internal" control of manpower. But that balance was disrupted during the war when international migration was seriously curtailed.

As discussed in chapter 2, until the decade of 1910–20, the rate of migration to the United States remained at high levels, subject only to fluctuations associated with the business cycle there. At the same time black migration from the South remained at relatively low levels, at least as compared to the level experienced starting in 1910–20. Once immigration declined, however, there was a dramatic pickup in the South to North movement of African Americans. In excess of 350,000 African Americans are estimated to have departed from the six plantation states during the 1910s. This figure must have been largely concentrated in the second half of the decade, and represents more than a doubling of the number of blacks who left the plantation south in any of the immediately preceding decades. In the 1920s the rapid pace of outmigration of blacks continued with nearly 700,000 African Americans estimated as having vacated the six plantation states in these years.[2]

Although push factors—specifically the boll weevil infestation which damaged the 1915 crop—were operative, the timing of this population movement suggests that it was the pull of the demand for labor in the North which principally accounted for the magnitude of this "Great Migration."[3] In the absence of new immigrant workers, northern firms flooded the South with recruiters seeking to hire blacks. Initially the response to these recruiting efforts was tepid, but by 1916 the number of black migrants swelled. Railroad recruiters arrived in the South in that same year, resulting in the Pennsylvania Railroad alone bringing 12,000 blacks north to maintain track and equipment.[4] In excess of one million African Americans migrated from the six plantation states during the decades of the 1910s and 1920s. As Neil McMillen has written on migration from Mississippi, "with normal sources of cheap, white immigrant labor disrupted and the nation's labor needs sharply accelerated by the draft and industrial expansion, Afro-Americans who were once welcome in the urban North only in personal service occupations now found themselves in demand as unskilled and semiskilled industrial workers."[5] In Richard A. Easterlin's words, "with the foreign labor supply largely cut off, periods of high labor demand in the North began increasingly to generate large movements of blacks out of the South."[6]

In his vivid portrayal of the Great Migration James R. Grossman agrees with E. Franklin Frazier in describing it as the "second emancipation." This characterization follows from the fact that the movement North "drew upon black Southerners who looked to urban life and the industrial economy for the social and economic foundation of full citizenship and its perquisites." As such the second emancipation required that the African American population undertake the wrenching community, worklife, and cultural changes which are associated with the shift from farm to factory. Seen in another light, therefore, the Great Migration represented the collapse of the hope that freedom could be found through landownership in the rural South. The move from the South was the clearest possible expression of the fact that the African American population was giving up on the South and was anxious to escape the confines of the plantation way of life. Important in this regard was the nature of industrial, as contrasted to plantation, employment. African Americans reacted favorably to the absence of the paternalism of plantation life in the North. Grossman quotes a migrant as celebrating that "I can quit any time I want to," and comments that what seems to have been critical is that in the North "distant employers, unlike landlords or merchants with a lien on the crop, neither pressured wives and children to work [nor were concerned with] what blacks did outside the workplace." Nonwork hours belonged to the African Americans themselves, rather than being subject to continuous planter supervision and control, as had been the case in the plantation South. Not surprisingly the movement north encountered considerable opposition from southern black leaders, particularly those associated with the thinking of Booker T. Washington. Furthermore it did not take southern black migrants long to learn that the freedom they experienced in the North was badly flawed and therefore bitterly disappointing. Nonetheless

W. E. B. DuBois captured the options available to African Americans in the United States when he wrote in 1920 that "the North is no paradise, but the South is at best a system of caste and insult and at worst a Hell."[7]

The single most important spokesperson calling for the northward flow of black labor was Robert Abbott. Abbott was editor and publisher of the *Chicago Defender*, the most widely read and influential black newspaper during this period. Abbott founded the paper in 1905 in Chicago and from its beginning it crusaded against southern white supremacy. Although published in the North, the *Defender*, in the words of James R. Grossman, "penetrated into some of the most remote corners of the Black South." At first the paper advised black southerners to remain where they were. But when in 1916 employment opportunities for African Americans opened up in Chicago, the *Defender* adopted a new position and encouraged migration. Abbott argued in the pages of the paper that "our problem today is to widen our economic opportunities, to find more openings and more kinds of openings in the industrial world. Our chance is right now." He urged blacks to "come North where there is more humanity, some justice and fairness."[8] The paper, according to Florette Henry, "in news items, anecdotes, cartoons and photos . . . crystallized immediate motives for flight."[9] Indeed the *Defender* directly promoted the migration by choosing May 15, 1917 as the date for the Great Northern Drive. Although there was no organization established to provide transportation to the North on that date, nonetheless, in Grossman's words, "many migrants did conceive of their actions as part of a mass movement."[10] The *Defender*'s position could not have been clearer. It declared that:

> . . . anywhere in God's country is far better than the Southland. Every black man for the sake of his wife and daughters especially should leave even at a financial sacrifice every spot in the South where his worth is not appreciated enough to give him the standing of a man and a citizen in the community. We know full well that this would mean a depopulation of that section and if it were possible we would glory in its accomplishment.[11]

The Great Migration suggests that the African American population believed migration from the South was the most realistic option available to improve its standard of living. In the suffocating context of the plantation economy it was not likely that the kind of training and self-help advocated by Washington would adequately widen the space for economic advance in the South. Further there were no signs of the kinds of political breakthroughs which DuBois insisted were prerequisite for economic success in that region. With the prognosis in the South unfavorable, a positive response to the change in the northern labor market must have seemed the most reasonable response available to African Americans.

While migration thus may have been the most promising option available, there were important shortcomings associated with it as well; two in particular loom as decisive. The first was the continuing legacy of racism in the North. To employer hostility was now added increased tension with the white working class. Black labor, when recruited to northern employment opportunities, often was expected to act as strikebreakers. The resulting conflicts with white workers created, in the words of William Julius Wilson, "incidents that [both] dramatically revealed and directly contributed to a racially charged atmosphere."[12] The second shortcoming was that African American migrants were handicapped by their limited entrepreneurial experience. Small business ownership is a potentially effective way to advance in a market context. Yet overwhelmingly landlessness in the South had deprived the black population of entrepreneurial experience. As Thomas Sowell has noted, "one of the remarkable characteristics of American Negroes has been the relative smallness of their business class compared to that of other ethnic groups."[13] Thus black economic advance in the North, as had been the case in the South, could receive very little assistance from black businesses.

Although the Great Migration represented a means to escape from the oppression of the plantation economy, it was by no means the case that it would result in successful integration in the North. Racism in employment, education, and housing manifested itself in the northern cities to which African Americans had relocated. Because of this the group solidarity present as the black population mobilized itself for the movement to the North was required there as well as in the South.

The ghettoized and deprived conditions which confronted blacks in the North suggested at least to some African Americans that further efforts at advance within the United States were futile. For these individuals a search for a black home outside the country was imperative. Such an approach was offered by Marcus Garvey. Garvey's politics evolved over a period of time, but a full statement of his mature views appeared in 1923. He rejected the position which "sought to teach the Negro to aspire to social equality with whites," arguing that "this has been the source of much trouble." Instead, he went on, "the time is opportune to regulate the relationship between both races. Let the Negro have a country of his own. Help him to return to his original home, Africa, and there give him the opportunity to climb from the lowest to the highest positions in a state of his own."[14] The Garvey position neatly combined self-help sensibilities, the demonstrated mobility of the black population, and the frustration and despair generated by the racial animus in the North into a comprehensive separatism. In the Garveyite formulation self-help had become nationhood, migration had become a return to the "original home," Africa—both fueled by the unwillingness of the people of the United States to treat black people as equals.

By about 1920 Garvey's United Negro Improvement Association (UNIA), with its combined advocacy of solidarity and mobility, had become the most important black organization in the country. However this movement never did identify a place in Africa to which the African American people could relocate. Nevertheless the Garveyite movement was successful in mobilizing large numbers of followers. As Harold Cruse puts it:

> . . . adopting what he wanted from Washington's ideas, Garvey carried them further—advocating Negro self-sufficiency in the United States linked this time, with the idea of regaining access to the African homeland as a basis for constructing a viable black economy.[15]

DuBois stood in opposition to the Garveyite movement, as he had to Booker T. Washington's exclusive reliance on self-help. The main point of contention in this context was the nature of the African homeland, an especially important argument since DuBois was a pan-Africanist, although in a very different manner than Garvey. Garvey's biographer, Elton C. Fax, described their differences well:

> Both DuBois and Garvey were Pan-Africanists. The difference separating them was this: DuBois' Pan-Africanism was designed as an aid to African national self-determination under African leadership for the benefit of Africans themselves. Garvey's Pan-Africanism envisioned the movement as one in which Africa would be the place where black peoples of the Western world would colonize and there Garvey and his U.N.I.A. would head the program of Colonization, with the consent and cooperation of African leaders.[16]

In addition to their contrasting views about Africa, DuBois and Garvey sharply disagreed—in a manner reminiscent of the DuBois-Washington disagreement—over the utility of political struggle in the United States. Garvey simply did not accept DuBois's belief in the efficacy of efforts to achieve social and political equality in the United States. Such actions, in his view, were doomed to failure because "reason dictates that the masses of the white race will never stand by the ascendency of an opposite minority group to favored positions in a government, society and industry that exists by the will of the majority." He warned that "the demand of the DuBois group of colored leaders will only lead ultimately to further disturbances in riots, lynchings and mob rule."[17] Political involvement was fruitless. Garvey argued that the only logical solution to the plight of the black population was emigration.

The Garveyite movement was relatively short-lived. It had shrunk in size considerably by the time Garvey himself was deported from the United States in 1927. Despite its rapid demise, however, the Garveyite ideology represented a major new departure in black thinking. With Garvey the sense of self and community, which had previously supported the self-help concept, now received a more complete expression as nationhood. The black experience was sufficiently similar over the entire African American population, reasoned Garvey, that it cemented individuals together culturally as well as economically. From this commonality a nation could be forged. In the Garvey formulation the locus of this nation was Africa. But more important than the geographic location of the nation was that Garvey had given expression to and mobilized a following around the nationalism which had always been latent in self-help but which the spokespersons for the latter had rejected.

In the end, however, the demise of Garveyism meant that the nationalist position had not been accepted by the bulk of the African American population. It is true that the Communist party in 1928 adopted a position affirming the right of black belt self-determination. Even so, however, the Communist party in practice tended not to emphasize this position, instead tending to concentrate on trade union and antidiscrimination activities.[18] Instead of pursuing what in all likelihood would have been a protracted and ultimately futile struggle for a geographic entity of its own, the black population during the 1930s adopted a politics which identified its interests with that of the people of the broader polity of the country. This integrationist aspiration was signalled by the very strong support it provided to the New Deal, a dramatic departure from its long pattern of voting for the Republican party. In effect the black population had decided that given the options available, its best hope was to attempt to share the economic well-being generated once growth was resumed in the country.

The impact of the Great Migration was not limited to the black population. It also possessed potentially disruptive consequences for the South and its plantation economy. The chain of causality could have begun with the labor scarcities and potential bottlenecks to production caused by the outward movement, given the labor-intensive cultivation techniques employed in cotton. These scarcities, in their turn, might have vested in the labor force enhanced bargaining power—both in a probable upward trend in incomes and in the leverage planters exercised over black tenants in social relations. The planter's inability to impose a new juridical slavery, combined with increasing costs and declining availability of labor, might have threatened not only the cultural paternalism of the plantation economy but also its profits. In short a massive and continuous movement north might have confronted the planters with a breakdown of the plantation economy as a way of life.[19]

The disruption in the plantation economy which might have occurred if migration had continued on the scale of that seen in the 1920s was, however, delayed. African American migration from the South fell by more than 50 percent in the 1930–40 decade compared to the 1920–30 period. Whereas about 749,000 blacks left the South in the earlier decade, that number fell to 347,000 in the later.[20] Because of this decline, the labor scarcity which would have undermined the plantation economy was not experienced, and plantation agriculture persisted for another decade.

However, the black migration of 1910–40 did mean that the demographic composition of the plantation-dominated counties of the South changed substantially. Because of the outmigration the absolute number of African Americans in those counties actually fell by 3.7 percent between 1910 and 1930. The slowdown in migration in the 1930s meant that the size of the black population in the plantation counties reached about the same level in 1940 that it had in 1910. In the meantime the white population continued a slow but steady increase, so that the proportion of African Americans in the population steadily declined from almost 55 percent in 1910 to about 45 percent

Table 20   Black Population of 270 Southern Plantation Counties, 1910–40

	Total Population	Black Population	% Black
1910	7,195,600	3,393,627	54.7
1920	7,683,842	3,844,758	50.0
1930	8,256,808	3,789,093	45.9
1940	8,822,938	4,005,465	45.4

Sources: Appendix (this book); U.S. Bureau of the Census [census for each year].

Table 21   Sources of Productivity Growth in Wheat, Corn, and Cotton Production, 1920–40 (in percentages)

	Wheat	Corn	Cotton
Decrease in man-hours*	46.0	26.5	32.0
Decrease in man-hours per acre	37.5	21.9	−8.9
Change in output per acre	15.2	6.7	37.7

Source: See table 10.
*Per 100 bushels of wheat or corn and 500 pound-bales of cotton.

in 1940 (Table 20). But while the demographic composition of the plantation counties did show some change, the fundamentals of plantation agriculture remained intact. In particular mechanization in cotton continued to lag behind the pace experienced in other comparable but nonplantation crops. Overall labor productivity in cotton advanced more slowly than in wheat, but more rapidly than in corn between 1920 and 1940. However as indicated in Table 21, labor requirements per acre (my proxy for mechanization) in cotton actually increased during this period, precisely the opposite of what would have been recorded if mechanization were underway. This means that although cultivation techniques had improved as evidenced by increased yields, as yet the obstacles to mechanization in plantation cultivation had not been eliminated.

The Great Depression clearly interfered with the demise of the plantation economy promised by the outmigration of African Americans from the South. The general prosperity of the 1920s and the legislatively limited flow of immigrants to the United States was responsible for black outmigration. But the high rates of unemployment experienced during the Depression meant that the opportunity fell substantially for black migrants successfully to find nonagricultural work in the North. As a result the labor force base necessary to sustain plantation agriculture still was present in the South.

Data on northern unemployment by race are not available for the years before 1940. Thus the deprivation experienced specifically by the African American population in that region during the Depression cannot systematically be examined. Nonetheless a sampling of the available data provides an impression of the severity of the impact of the Depression on the urban black labor force, thus offering insight into the decline in African American migration from the South during the decade of the 1930s. According to the Federal Emergency Relief Administration in 1933 the proportion of urban blacks on relief stood at 26.7 percent, almost three times the level for urban whites. The Urban League learned that in some cases the percentage on relief was even higher. For example in Cleveland this figure stood at 33 percent; it was 37 percent in Detroit, and 30 percent in Chicago. Although these data do not give a complete picture of the extent of poverty, it nonetheless seems clear that economic life for urban blacks was devastated. As Mary Ellison put it these data on the extent of relief in fact probably show "only the tip of the iceberg of the actual amount of destitution."[21] The pattern is clear. Real deprivation was experienced by African Americans moving from the South to the North during the 1930s. For many new migrants the promise of freedom in the North therefore turned out to be a disappointment. The entrapment and poverty associated with the plantation economy in the South had been traded for the confinement of involuntary unemployment and its associated poverty in the North. As a result the movement of African Americans was sharply curtailed.

Again in the 1930s, as in earlier periods, conditions outside of the South permitted a continuation of the plantation economy. In this case the Depression and the resultant immiserization of northern urban blacks seem to have slowed the process of black migration sufficiently to allow for continued plantation viability. Nonetheless the plantation structure was very weak. The abundance of labor required by plantation agriculture was available only because the demand for workers in the North had collapsed. If that demand had remained

Table 22 Plantations by Acres under Cultivation, 1934

	Total Cultivated Acreage							
	<200	200–400	400–600	600–800	800–1000	1000–1200	≥1200	Total
# of Plantations	241	213	81	42	29	15	25	646
% of Plantations	37.3	33.0	12.5	6.5	4.5	2.3	3.9	100.0

Source: T. J. Woofter, Jr., *Landlord and Tenant on the Cotton Plantation* (Washington, D.C.: Division of Social Research, Works Progress Administration, 1936), p. 40.

strong it well could have been the case that plantation agriculture no longer would have been viable; indeed the demise of the plantation economy awaited only the return of a tight labor market in the North.

But while the decline in migration from the plantation South in the 1930s compared to the 1920s extended the life of plantation cultivation, it is significant that even in the 1930s a substantial black migration from the South persisted. Indeed this South to North flow in the 1930s was comparable to that in the 1910s and larger than any decade previous to that point. Thus the question remains why in spite of the collapse of the Northern labor market did African Americans continue to leave the South at a time when economic prospects in the North were anything but favorable? One hypothesis centers on the possibility that black incomes in the urban North, despite the difficulties encountered there, were higher than those in the plantation South. Direct observations useful in testing this hypothesis are not available for this period, but it is possible to obtain a rough estimate of the magnitudes involved by using data collected by the Division of Social Research of the Works Progress Administration in 1934. T. J. Woofter and his associates carried out a survey of 646 plantations concentrated in the 6 plantation states of Alabama, Arkansas, Georgia, Louisiana, Mississippi, and South Carolina, and also included about 30 plantations in North Carolina. Tenant families on these plantations totaled 9,215 or about 14 per plantation. More than half of the plantations were relatively small with less than 10 families resident. Only about 10 percent contained more than 30 families (see Table 22).

Data provided in the survey allow us to estimate income per tenant family (see table 23 for the method of estimation). Not surprisingly these estimates reveal very low levels of income for most

Table 23   Estimating Operator and Tenant Net Income, 1934

1. Plantation Net Income − Operator Net Income = Tenant Net Income
$$\$3,885,742 - \$1,659,082 = \$2,226,660$$

2. Tenant Net Income ÷ Number of Plantations = Tenant Net Income per plantation
$$\$2,226,660 \div 646 = \$3,447$$

3. Operator Net Income ÷ Number of Plantations = Operator Net Income per plantation
$$\$1,659,082 \div 646 = \$2,568$$

4. Tenant Net Income per Plantation ÷ Tenants per Plantation = Net Income per Tenant Family
$$\$3,447 \div 14.3 = \$241$$

Source: Calculated from T. J. Woofter, Jr., *Landlord and Tenant on the Cotton Plantation* (Washington, D.C.: Division of Social Research, Works Progress Administration, 1936), pp. 69, 77, 78.

Table 24   Sources of Sharecropper Income, 1934 (in dollars)

Cash Items	122
Cash after utility	91
Wages	21
Agricultural Adjustment Act	8
Unshared sales	2
Noncash Items	190
Subsistence advances	85
Home-use production	105
Total Net Income	312

Source: T. J. Woofter, Jr., *Landlord and Tenant on the Cotton Plantation* (Washington, D.C.: Division of Social Research, Works Progress Administration, 1936), 87.

participants in the plantation economy. Estimated operator income, for example, was more than ten times the level of income received by tenants. Furthermore as revealed in Table 24 at least 60 percent of sharecropper income was received on a noncash basis in the form of subsistence advances and home use production. Thus these 1934 data suggest that sharecropper annual family cash income averaged only about $122 per year.

Obviously income levels for employed black workers in the urban North were higher than this. For example the median household income for black families in New York at approximately the same time came to $980. In Chicago the median was $726. Low as these figures were they still meant that the migration north promised a substantial increase in incomes over that received by tenants in the plantation economy, provided, of course, that employment could be found.[22]

In the meantime the advantage that the South might have possessed over the North—namely, that at least there were jobs available on the plantations, no matter how low wages might be—was also disappearing. Particularly important in this regard was the implementation of New Deal agricultural policies starting with the Agricultural Adjustment Act (AAA) of 1932. Faced in 1932 with the "pathetic price" of 5 cents per pound of cotton and a three year inventory of the crop, AAA policy was to pay farmers to plow under one-fourth of the cotton crop. By so doing it was anticipated that prices would rise, and inventories decline. The combination of the stronger commodity market resulting from the induced scarcity and the subsidies paid to the farmers to withhold production, it was believed, would substantially increase incomes earned in cotton cultivation.

There is a consensus in the historical literature that in the administration of the AAA the interests of plantation tenants were relegated to a relatively low status compared to those of the planters. The result was that this New Deal program cost many tenants their livelihood. The problem was to decide if, under the terms of the law, sharecroppers and tenants were entitled to receive benefits or if they were merely laborers paid with a share of the crop and therefore not entitled to such compensation. At the beginning of the program, in 1933, the contracts issued specified that benefit payments were to be divided in accordance with the share of the crop, a procedure beneficial to the croppers. But according to Whatley "many landlords were not satisfied with their share under the plow-up program and resented those 'government people' breaking tradition by sending checks directly to croppers." As a result in subsequent contracts the legal claim croppers had to benefits under the program was substantially weakened.[23]

Once it was established that payments for withholding land from production were predominantly to be received by landlords and not tenants, it was certain that there would be a reduction in the cropper labor force in cotton. As Conrad has written:

About 50 percent of the landlord's acreage lay fallow and yet if he kept the same number of tenants his operating expenses for the year would be almost as great. If he evicted tenants he would not have to support them, he would not have to split government benefit money with them, and he would use the rented acres for his own purposes.[24]

Furthermore the benefit formula employed tended also to be adverse to croppers.[25] An acre taken out of cultivation from a cropper was compensated less than one taken from a wage system. Thus both the system of benefit payments and the benefit schedules themselves were deleterious to cropper interests. On one hand that the AAA benefits predominantly were received by planters meant that they had a clear incentive to reduce their labor force. On the other hand differential compensation meant that those same planters possessed an incentive to replace croppers with wage workers.

Thus in addition to the pull of possible higher living standards in the North there was a push of black laborers from the South. Indeed it appears likely that during these years the relative strength of one compared to the other may have changed. The push may have intensified while the pull may have declined because of mounting northern unemployment. In combination these two forces resulted in a decline in the number of black sharecroppers in the South from 393,000 in 1930 to 299,000 in 1940. Black nonshare tenantry also declined in these years, with the number of such renters in the South falling from 306,000 to 208,000.[26]

Although the plantation economy persisted through the 1930s its vulnerability had intensified. The migration shook the southern way of life because apart from its direct effect on the plantation labor supply, it demonstrated to those who stayed behind that an alternative way of life was possible. If conditions in the urban North were hardly satisfactory, they nonetheless represented an improvement over life on plantations. Furthermore the presence of migrants in the North made it easier for the latecomers to make the trek from the South. By establishing a network of friends and relations mobility was facilitated. To the extent that the network grew the props supporting the plantation economy were undermined.

Related to this was the fact that the migration broke down the remoteness of the South and brought to national attention the plight of those who continued to labor within the plantation economy. Sharecropping and segregation, writes Nicholas Lemann, were "just as much a thing apart from the mainstream of American life as slavery had been" and had lasted just about as long as slavery had.[27] But the work of scholars centered at the University of North Carolina during the 1930s and 1940s—such as Rupert Vance, Charles S. Johnson and T. J. Woofter—tended to break down this isolation and bring conditions in the South to the attention of policymakers and the public. Although difficult to estimate with precision, the contribution made by these scholars in educating the American people to conditions in the plantation South—and thus making them more receptive to later civil rights efforts—seems real and significant. Obviously, however, the light shed on the plantation system through scholarship did not result in immediate changes. Such change could be expected only when the principal actors in southern society mobilized themselves to behave in ways inconsistent with the smooth functioning of the plantation economy.

Thus an even more significant promise of change during the 1930s was to be found in the organizing initiatives undertaken by black farmers themselves. Probably the most important of these organizations was the Southern Tenant Farmers' Union (STFU). Organized in 1934 the STFU was multiracial and by 1936 contained 10,000 black members out of a total membership of 31,000. Supported by both the NAACP and Norman Thomas' Socialist Party, the STFU fought for direct governmental subsidy payments to tenants rather than landlords and also struggled against cropper evictions.[28] In Alabama a sharecropper union was organized with similar goals, although perhaps a lesser degree of success. The strength of the commitment to such organizations by African Americans is revealed in Nate Shaw's autobiography. In Shaw's case the threat of eviction stirred indignation to the point of heroism. In the act of defending the farm and property of a neighbor, Shaw was arrested, tried, convicted, and served ten years in prison.[29] The stirring of collective self defense, represented by organizations such as the STFU and epitomized by Shaw's story, signals the rejection of the paternalistic ethos present in the plantation South. However, the full flowering of this rejection of the plantation way of life awaited the birth of the southern civil rights movement.

The period between World War I and 1940 was one in which an incremental chipping away at the structure of the plantation economy occurred. The structure remained intact with the planters continuing to control large numbers of dependent workers in the cultivation of the cotton staple. Below the surface, however, large numbers of African Americans resident in the South had learned or were learning the route by which to escape the plantation economy, while others were learning to resist the paternalistic impositions of the plantation regime through collective action. All the while the plantation structure was coming under increased scrutiny. These years, in short, represented a period in which the plantation economy had come to be seen by increasing numbers of southern blacks and their potential allies elsewhere as an anachronism, the structure of which could be attacked either indirectly by migration or frontally through political or union efforts.

The Collapse of
the Plantation Economy

7

The entry of the United States into World War II marks the principal point of discontinuity in the black experience in this country. Until then participation in the southern plantation economy had remained the single most important economic activity of the African American population. From this participation followed the fact that most blacks were southern, rural, and poor. Now with the major social mobilization associated with the war, masses of African American workers were required either directly or indirectly to support the war effort. This intense need for black labor provided a renewed opportunity for large numbers of plantation tenants to migrate. Black migration from the six plantation states during the 1940s totaled in excess of one million individuals, a number almost three times that of the 1930s decade and a magnitude far greater than the African American migration of any previous decade.[1] By any standard this was a movement of major demographic significance. In its turn the migration triggered the long-delayed mechanization of cotton cultivation. With World War II, in short, the South's plantation economy, based as it was on the availability of cheap black labor, was once and for all shattered.

In principle a loss in population of this magnitude could either be the result of a reduction in the demand for agricultural labor in the South or a reduction in the supply of such labor, perhaps because of an increased demand for it elsewhere. Data on wage rates are useful in trying to choose between these two explanations. An increase in labor costs at the time of the outmigration would suggest that what was operative was a pull mechanism, resulting in labor scarcity. Alternatively an absence of such upward pressure on wages would suggest the presence of a push mechanism. In this case labor loss would not have caused a scarcity, suggesting that the demand for labor had fallen.

The wage data available makes it clear that labor was leaving the South primarily because it was attracted to employment opportunities elsewhere. The United States Department of Labor reports that in 1946 the cost of labor in cotton picking averaged 7 cents a pound. This figure represented a substantial increase from the level of about 1 cent

Table 25   Distribution of Blacks by Occupation and Sex, 1940–44 (in percentages)

	Males			Females		
	1940	1944	Change	1940	1944	Change
Farmers	41.2	28.0	−13.2	16.0	8.1	−7.9
Industrial	17.0	29.7	12.7	6.5	18.0	11.5
Laborers	21.4	20.3	−1.1	0.8	2.0	1.2
Service	15.3	15.1	−0.2	70.3	62.5	−7.8
Clerical and sales	2.0	3.0	1.0	1.4	3.9	2.5
Proprietors, managers, and professionals	3.1	3.7	0.6	5.0	5.5	0.5

Source: "War and Post-War Trends in Employment of Negroes," *Monthly Labor Review* (January 1945).

a pound which prevailed during the 1930s.[2] Such strong upward pressure on labor costs is strong evidence that the loss in population did not result from a reduced demand for labor. Almost certainly, southern agriculture experienced a decline in the availability of labor consequent upon that labor force's responding to new employment opportunities in the North.

The key to this was the change which occurred in the demand for black labor during World War II. That this change was dramatic is made clear by comparing the occupational structure of the African American labor force in 1944 with that in 1940 (Table 25). The percentage of African American men who worked as farmers in one form or another fell in these four years from over 41 percent to 28 percent. This decline in farm work was almost perfectly matched by the increase in industrial employment. As a result of this shift to factory work, African American men represented 10.1 percent of all factory workers in 1944, almost a doubling from the 5.9 percent they represented in 1940 (Table 26).

A similar but not identical pattern of change occurred in African American female employment. In this case two categories of work fell noticeably. One of course was agricultural work. The other was service employment, the category which includes domestic service workers. Increases occurred in all other occupational categories for black

Table 26   Percentage of Blacks among Total Workers by
Occupational Group and Sex, 1940–44

	Males		Females	
	1940	1944	1940	1944
Professional and semiprofessional	2.8	3.3	4.5	5.7
Managers, officials, and proprietors	1.1	2.1	2.6	4.8
Clerical	1.6	3.5	0.7	1.6
Sales	1.1	1.5	1.2	1.1
Craftsmen, foremen	2.6	3.6	2.2	5.2
Operatives	5.9	10.1	4.7	8.3
Domestic service	60.2	75.2	46.6	60.9
Protective service	2.4	1.7	3.8	—
Personal service	22.8	31.4	12.7	24.0
Farmers, farm managers	12.4	11.0	30.4	23.8
Farm laborers	21.0	21.1	62.0	21.4
Laborers	21.0	27.6	13.2	35.6
Total	8.6	9.8	13.8	12.9

Source: See table 25.

women. However as was the case for men it was the expansion in
industrial employment which absorbed the bulk of the workers from
the declining categories. It is of interest to note that despite their
movement out of domestic service employment, African American
women represented 60.9 percent of all domestic workers in 1944,
compared to only 46.6 percent in 1940. This indicates that white
women moved out of this occupation even more rapidly than did black
women. In contrast, however, the shift from agricultural work by
African American women was more rapid than that of whites. In this
case the change was quite dramatic. Black women in 1944 constituted
only 21.4 percent of female agricultural workers compared to 62.0
percent in 1940. The change in the share of black women acting as
operatives was also considerable, although not as substantial as that
in farming; the percentage of African American females acting as operatives increased from 4.7 percent to 8.3 percent. By 1944 almost 10
percent of all factory positions were filled by blacks, representing just

Table 27   Distribution of Blacks by Industry and Sex, 1940–44
(in percentages)

Industry	Males		Females	
	1940	1944	1940	1944
Agriculture	42.0	29.9	16.1	8.1
Forestry, fishing	0.8	0.5	—	—
Mining	1.8	4.2	—	—
Construction	4.9	3.7	0.1	—
Manufacturing	16.2	23.9	3.2	13.4
Metals, chemicals, rubber	5.5	13.1	0.2	7.3
Food, clothing, textiles, leather	2.8	4.7	1.8	3.9
Other	7.9	6.1	1.2	2.2
Transportation, communications, public utilities	6.8	10.1	0.2	1.1
Trade	9.9	10.9	4.0	10.5
Finance, insurance, real estate	1.9	1.6	0.8	1.3
Business and repair service	1.7	1.5	0.1	0.1
Domestic and personal service	8.4	6.1	68.6	54.4
Amusement, recreation	1.0	0.4	0.3	0.4
Professional services	2.9	3.2	6.1	7.5
Government	1.7	4.0	0.5	3.2
Total	100.0	100.0	100.0	100.0

Source: See table 25.

about a doubling of the African American representation in this occupational category.

The importance of the war in producing these rapid changes is indicated in Table 27. There the data indicate how important the munitions industries were in absorbing African American labor. The category which shows the largest increase in black workers—metals, chemicals, and rubber—included the principal war industries such as iron and steel, machinery, and aircraft and shipbuilding. According to the Bureau of Labor Statistics, "the actual number of Negro men in this group increased by well over a quarter of a million between 1940 and 1944, tripling in four years."[3]

The employment advances achieved by African Americans during the war, however, did not come easily or automatically. Robert C.

Weaver has detailed how, even in the face of critical labor shortages, racially discriminatory hiring and promotion practices persisted in major industrial centers. Furthermore the pattern of discrimination also persisted in job and vocational training programs, thus limiting the availability of black labor for skilled trades. As Mary Ellison has written, it still was the case that "Black labor everywhere was under-used and misused during the war."[4]

The combination of wartime patriotism and tight labor markets created an environment in which black protests against discrimination were particularly effective. Representatives of the African American community were able to point to the hypocrisy of fighting a war in the name of democracy abroad while practicing racism domestically. At the same time it was also possible to point out that the labor short-ages caused by discrimination hindered the war effort itself. In this context the threat by A. Philip Randolph, the leader of the largely black union of Sleeping Car Porters, to mount a protest rally in Wash-ington in 1941 was instrumental in inducing the Roosevelt Admin-istration to issue an executive order barring discrimination in defense industries and appointing the first Fair Employment Practice Com-mission.[5] At times this struggle was also joined by sympathetic unions, especially those affiliated with the CIO. The war was respon-sible for the convergence of the national interest and the interest of the black labor force. As the wartime Manpower Commission put it, "we cannot afford the luxury of thinking in terms of white men's work. It isn't white men's work we had to do—it's war work and there's more than enough of it."[6]

The changes that occurred in the demand for nonagricultural black labor during the war apparently were widely perceived among African American enlisted men. A study of postwar migration plans carried out in 1944 found that proportionately twice as many blacks as whites anticipated relocating after the war.[7] Black soldiers expected, in large numbers, to move from the South. In short they did not anticipate that the war-induced changes in the demand for black labor would be reversed. Rather they felt that employment opportunities would continue to be available to them in the North.

This optimism about the postwar demand for black labor was not universally shared. Once before, during the 1930s, occupational advance for African Americans had been curtailed, and it was far from certain that such a pattern would not reappear. This threat loomed all the more alarmingly since many feared that an economic downturn

Table 28   Southern Sharecroppers by Race, 1930–59

	1930	1940	1945	1950	1954	1959
White	383,381	242,173	176,260	148,708	107,416	47,650
Nonwhite	392,897	299,118	270,296	198,057	160,246	73,387
Total	776,278	541,291	446,556	346,765	267,662	121,037
% Nonwhite	50.6	55.3	60.5	57.1	59.9	60.6

Source: U.S. Bureau of the Census, *Historical Statistics of the United States, Colonial Times to 1970*, part I, Series K109–153.

awaited the end of the war. The Bureau of Labor Statistics early sounded the warning. Noting that blacks had achieved their biggest advances "in those industries (especially the 'metals, chemicals and rubber' group) which will experience the greatest post war declines," and that by the rules of seniority blacks would be the first to be laid off in these industries, the Bureau warned that the wartime gains might be jeopardized if a contraction in the demand for nonagricultural labor were permitted in the postwar period. The bureau argued that "the consolidation of the Negro's gains in the postwar period . . . is dependent in large measure upon the volume of employment that then prevails."[8] In other words the war was responsible for the occupational gains achieved by black workers, but it was as yet unclear that those advances could be maintained.

If the future of African American labor in the North remained unclear, the plantation economy was doomed by the massive wartime migration by blacks.[9] Sharecropping was the means by which southern planters had assured themselves of abundant labor at the times of peak labor demand in cotton cultivation. The maintenance of a resident labor force on small producing units had militated against cotton mechanization. But the combination of both the AAA program, which pushed labor from the South and induced the increased use of wage labor, as well as the pull of northern employment opportunities had by the early 1940s undermined share tenantry. Between 1930 and 1940 the number of black southern sharecroppers declined by 23.9 percent (Table 28). With that decline the institution most responsible for the delay in farm mechanization had been weakened.

But the change in labor supply conditions had a significance over and above an increase in farm labor costs, and the decline in plantation tenantry. With the migration black agricultural workers who remained in the region were able to exercise increased selectivity in their choice of occupations. Seymour Melman, in his study of the mechanization process in cotton, reported that problems with the supply of labor had affected relations between planters and field hands. Melman quotes a delta planter as saying, "The day when a man could protect the grade of his cotton and assume a clean picked crop by threatening his labour with a single-tree or a trace chain has gone forever. The word spreads fast against that kind of planter nowadays and first thing he knows he can't get anybody to pick his cotton."[10]

The significance of such a change in management-labor relations in the plantation South can scarcely be overestimated. The plantation economy rested not merely on limited alternatives, but also upon deference. It was dependency as well as control which characterized the organization of production. The low wages which had always prevailed in the region reflected not merely labor abundance and low levels of labor productivity, but cultural and political subordination as well. It was this—black subservience—which was uprooted by the black migration from the region. With the heightened bargaining power that migration vested in the remaining plantation workers and tenants, deference became increasingly anachronistic and irrelevant. In turn labor market relations began, for the first time, to resemble real negotiations.

The response by the planters to this breakdown in the props underlying the plantation economy constituted the first serious attempt to revolutionize production methods by adopting mechanized methods of cultivation and harvesting. With labor increasingly scarce and expensive, with the decline of sharecropping and with the former social subordination of their labor force now in jeopardy, the system of incentives facing the planters regarding the choice of production methods had been irreversibly altered. The breakdown of share tenantry meant that labor cost savings could be achieved incrementally; with the increased cost of farm labor, moreover, there was an urgency to do so. Planters now found that it was increasingly cost-effective to mechanize production.

Specifically the focus of attention was directed to the harvest. According to Gavin Wright mechanization was greatly accelerated during the war, "but throughout the decade cotton farmers were unable to complete the mechanization process for one specific reason: the harvest bottleneck."[11] There had been a long history of experimentation with regard to mechanical cotton harvesters and by the

Table 29   U.S. Production of Spindle-Type Cotton Picking
Machines, 1946–53

Year	Number
1946 and earlier	107
1947	649
1948	766
1949	901
1950	1,527
1951	3,419
1952	4,509
1953	3,741

Source: James H. Street, *The New Revolution in the Cotton Economy: Mechanization and Its Consequences* (Chapel Hill: The University of North Carolina Press, 1957), p. 133

early 1930s an effective one had been developed. During these early years, however, demand for the harvester was limited, constrained by the continued disincentives to mechanization associated with share-cropping and the relatively low cost of labor. As a result few firms devoted much attention or many resources to perfecting harvester design.[12] During World War II, of course, these market signals reversed and increasingly producers had an incentive to develop and planters to purchase this technology. The exigencies of the war, however, prevented firms such as International Harvester from turning their attention fully to the production and sale of this equipment and satisfying this newfound demand.

According to James Street the fact that International Harvester was ready to enter into commercial production, coupled with increasing demand, "stimulated a race on the part of other implement firms to get into the market with a similar picker." By the end of the 1940s Deere and Company and Allis Chalmers Manufacturing Company both entered the market with mechanical pickers. Initially the high price of these machines precluded their use for all but the largest and wealthiest cotton growers. By the early 1950s, however, a model appeared at about one-half the initial price, and, as a result, the sale of mechanical pickers increased substantially. Table 29 reports Street's data on the sale of mechanical picking machines during this period, demonstrating the explosive growth which occurred during these years.[13]

Table 30   Man-Hour Levels in Cotton Production, 1920–60

	1920	1940	1950	1960
Man-hours/acre	90	98	74	54
Before harvest	55	46	33	23
After harvest	35	52	41	31
Yields of lint/acre (lbs.)	160	245	283	454
Man-hours/bale	269	191	126	57

Source: U.S. Bureau of the Census, *Historical Statistics of the United States, Colonial Times to 1970*, part I, Series K93-97 (Washington, D.C.: GPO, 1975).

The scope of what mechanization could accomplish was dramatic. The Bureau of Agricultural Statistics of the U.S. Department of Agriculture estimated that under mechanization, man-hours per bale of cotton could be reduced by about 80 percent compared to hand methods of harvesting the crop. By far the most substantial reduction in the required labor input occurred when the cotton boll was mechanically picked, although labor savings were feasible in other stages of cultivation as well.[14]

In addition to mechanization, productivity gains were achieved in other aspects of cotton cultivation. These gains included innovations in the application of fertilizer and improvements in methods of planting as well as insect control. These advances in cultivation techniques primarily increased yields per acre. These efforts were particularly successful during the 1950s. In that decade output per acre under cotton cultivation increased by slightly more than 60 percent (See Table 30).

Table 30 reveals the very sharp break which occurred in labor productivity trends in cotton between 1940 and 1950. As contrasted to the period between 1920 and 1940 when man-hours per acre actually increased, this proxy for mechanization fell dramatically during the 1940s. Disaggregating the measure into preharvest and harvest components again reveals the change in trend which occurred during these years. Between 1920 and 1940 man-hours per acre before the harvest had declined by 16.4 percent. In the ten years between 1940 and 1950 this same measure fell by 28.3 percent. While man-hours per acre in the harvest had actually increased between 1920 and 1940, that number fell by 21.2 percent in the 1940s. The upshot of these advances in mechanization is that in the ten years between 1940 and 1950 labor productivity in cotton (as measured by man-hours per bale) increased more than it had in the twenty years between 1920 and 1940.

It was in the 1940s, then, that technological change finally resulted in the demise of the plantation economy. The changes in production methods occurring during this period had themselves primarily been triggered by the increasing scarcity and cost of plantation labor during World War II.[15] Once black labor successfully began to escape the South, the planters were forced to face the fact that their traditional way of organizing production through the mobilization of a large number of dependent workers no longer was economically profitable or socially viable. What resulted was a reorganization of production, which by reducing the need for labor rendered anachronistic the institutions whose function had been to provide plantations with docile workers in large numbers. The paternalism and domination that characterized plantation cultivation now were superfluous.

World War II thus represented the beginning of a period of massive social change for the African American population in the United States. The black response to the wartime demand for labor simultaneously triggered the process of labor-displacing technological change in the South and dramatically increased the supply of black labor in the North. Although the escape from and dismantling of the plantation economy potentially symbolized enhanced economic opportunity, these changes were not without cost. Especially significant was that the potential represented by the movement North was not accompanied by the kind of public policy and planning necessary to ensure successful economic integration. The future of African Americans in the capitalist North was left largely to the labor market, without attention being directed either to ensuring that the skills possessed by the recent migrants fit the employment opportunities present in the North nor adjusting that pattern of labor demand to more nearly match the skills possessed by the newly arriving labor force.

With World War II the log jam at last was broken. After seven decades in which juridically free black labor was constrained to plantation agriculture because of the combined pressures of racist hiring practices in the North and South and economic depression, now, finally, in the 1940s, African American labor was urgently needed elsewhere. In response black workers fled the South and in so doing overwhelmed the mechanisms of control present in the region since Reconstruction. Thus the end of the plantation economy occurred in two steps. The first was the movement of black labor to the North in response to the pull of wartime labor requirements there. The second was the resulting technological changes which meant that cotton cultivators no longer required the extra-economic controls over their labor force, which had for so long been part of the plantation way of life.

Limited Economic Integration

8

During the three decades between 1940 and 1970 the geographic distribution of the African American population was fundamentally altered. African American migration from the South averaged almost 1.5 million people per decade in that thirty-year period. As a result the share of the black population resident in the South fell from 77 percent in 1940 to 53 percent in 1970. The migration North, furthermore, was overwhelmingly concentrated in the cities. Not only did the migrants become northerners, they also were transformed from a rural to an urban population. The percentage of the black population residing in rural areas in the United States in 1940 was 51 percent. By 1970 that percentage had declined to 19 percent.[1] Thus by the end of the decade of the 1960s a fundamental demographic redistribution of the black population had occurred.

With the huge migratory movement during and after World War II, the locus of the black economic experience in the United States had changed. While significant numbers remained in the South a rapidly increasing percentage of African Americans came to reside in the industrial centers of the North and West. This movement of people deeply affected the social structure of the South—doing no less than ending the southern plantation economy. At the same time it resulted in the settling of masses of black people in an unfamiliar economic environment. For those who remained in the South social relations had changed, while for those who moved North new circumstances were encountered.

In this dynamic context there emerged a new social movement with a new vision of equality for black people in the United States. In retrospect it is clear that the civil rights movement was for the most part a southern movement, addressing the inequities for blacks associated with the southern way of life. As Mary Ellison has written, Martin Luther King, Jr. "donated a philosophy and a certain easy eloquent style that gave voice to the mood of southern blacks."[2] But the South of the 1950s and 1960s was not the South of a former epoch. Indeed, it seems likely that the civil rights movement was born precisely because the South had begun to change.

The migratory movement which had started in the 1910s and swelled in the post-World War II era set in motion forces which fundamentally changed the structure of southern society. The demise of the plantation economy allowed for the initiation of a dynamic process of economic growth. As a result the demand for relatively high productivity labor increased, while the former mechanisms of labor control associated with plantation agriculture were increasingly irrelevant and anachronistic. The same forces that increased the demand for nonagricultural labor created conditions in which blacks found it easier to supply themselves for such employment opportunities.

The origins of the civil rights movement are to be found in the enhanced opportunities and capacities presented to African Americans in the context of rapid social change. As the authors of *A Common Destiny* point out, as labor-intensive agriculture declined wage levels and educational opportunities for southern blacks advanced, and these in turn facilitated the emergence of new and aggressive black community organizations.[3] At the same time the increasingly realistic possibility of social advance produced outrage at the social and legal constraints which continued to oppress southern blacks. Furthermore as the southern black population became increasingly mobile and involved in the industrial capitalist economy, deference as an acceptable stance toward society became increasingly unacceptable. The systematic discrimination which persisted in the South came to be seen as intolerable precisely as mobility and increased opportunity became real possibilities for large numbers of southern blacks. It also seems likely that the solidity of the opposition which African Americans confronted in their struggle for enhanced opportunity declined. The social changes experienced in the South meant that for increasing numbers of white southern leaders "the inadequacy of the black educational system and repression of black civil status represented an irrational underdevelopment of labor and consumer markets and a factor contributing to social disharmony."[4] The leaders of southern white society apparently divided into two groups: those who defended traditional southern constraints and those who identified with the needs of the modernizing southern economy. Those in the latter group tended to accept the breakdown of the old way of life in the interest of a more efficient social organization for which jim crow was not necessary.

It was, however, precisely because the civil rights movement preeminently addressed the vestiges of the plantation economy that it proved to have considerably less success in addressing the problems of African Americans in the North than in the South. The movement's major accomplishments were in the areas of the franchise, with the Voting Rights Act of 1965, the ending of officially sanctioned segregation in education following the 1954 Supreme Court decision in *Brown v. The Board of Education of Topeka,* a similar ban against discrimination in public accommodations in housing as mandated by the 1964 Civil Rights Act and the establishing of the Equal Employment Opportunities Commission also created by the 1964 act. Aside from discrimination in hiring, an issue which confronted African Americans throughout the country, the other victories largely were secured over predominantly southern practices. It was in the South that African Americans were disenfranchised, formally subjected to segregated education, and denied access to public accommodations. Even the color bar, although present everywhere, was more evident in the South than in the rest of the country. The civil rights movement was, in short, primarily southern in both its composition and accomplishments.

Seen in this way it is at once apparent how the civil rights movement was able to build the extensive coalition present, for example, at the 1963 Washington march, but at the same time failed to have much of an impact on the lives of the already ghettoized northern blacks. Segregation in the South provided a target against which a wide spectrum of northern support could mobilize. But because the archaic practices of the plantation economy were not operative elsewhere, and indeed were of decreasing relevance in the rapidly growing South of the 1960s, the impact of this movement was geographically confined. The riots which swept the northern urban areas during the 1960s served as testimony to the desperation which already prevailed in the North. But at the same time these events tended to point to the relative impotence of the civil rights movement in addressing the problems of the northern black population. The civil rights movement helped the South create an economy in which merit predominated over ascription. The black experience in the North established, however, that as important as that triumph might have been, it nonetheless was the case that a market system without racial barriers does not ensure racial equity.

Prosperity in a market setting such as prevailed in the North involves either filling an entrepreneurial role and benefiting from business profits, securing a professional occupation which yields a high income, or working as a highly productive worker in an occupation which pays substantial wages. Failing successfully to take one of these three routes means at best hard work and low income. But for African Americans the road to a higher standard of living was encumbered by problems of both demand and supply. On the demand side there remained the need to break down and destroy the long history, even in the North, of racial discrimination. These barriers were confronted not only in hiring but in access to the training and education essential to secure high-level employment. With regard to supply black life-styles and skills had been formed in the context of the plantation South and were appropriate to those circumstances. The plantation way of life, however, would have to be adjusted if migrants from the South were successfully to integrate into the society and economy of the industrial North. Richard Wright may have been referring to that necessity when he remarked "perhaps never in history has a more unprepared folk wanted to go to the city; we were barely born as a folk when we headed for the tall and sprawling centers of steel and stone."[5]

Its history of participation in the plantation economy meant that the black population left the South largely bereft of productive property. Overwhelmingly African Americans did not possess the source of substantial wealth under capitalism: ownership of assets for which they would be paid interest, dividends, profits, or royalties. As late as 1971 the profound differences by race in the ownership of productive property was manifest.[6] In that year blacks, representing about 11 percent of the population, received $53.3 billion or 6.9 percent of the total money income received by the population. However African Americans received only 0.9 percent of the total income paid in the form of dividends, interest, rents, and royalties. Similarly blacks received only 2.9 percent of nonfarm self-employed income and just 0.6 percent of farm self-employed income. When all such forms of property income are combined the total received by blacks comes to $1.9 billion or about 3.6 percent of total black income from all sources. By contrast property income as a percentage of all income came to 12.7 percent for whites. Thus property income proportionately was 3.5 times greater for whites than blacks.

Even within the category of property income, important differences by race show up. Of all the property income received by whites, 34.3 percent was in the form of dividends, interest, rent, and royalties, with the remainder coming from self-employment. By contrast only 15.8 percent of black property income came from interest, dividends, rents, and royalties. In short where blacks did receive property income it tended to result from their owning their own businesses. The continued marginalization of the black population from equity participation in the mainstream of the United States could not be more clear. Black businesses constituted an insignificantly small share of the country's economy, but nonetheless were almost exclusively the source of property income for the African American population.

Historically share tenantry denied entrepreneurial experience to African American agriculturalists. It is not surprising, therefore, that the first large-scale quantitative study of black businesses undertaken by Joseph Pierce in 1944 points to grave weaknesses. Pierce reported that slightly more than two-thirds of black businesses were in six service sectors: beauty parlors and barber shops (25.9 percent), eating places (19.1 percent), food stores (7.5 percent), cleaning and pressing (7.4 percent), shoe shine and repairs (4.7 percent), and funeral parlors (3.2 percent).[7] Similar subsequent studies showed a continued concentration in these service industries, a pattern which, according to Timothy Bates, indicated that "the black business community consisted of small scale operations concentrated in comparatively few lines of activity that offered little potential for growth."[8] Even compared to other minority groups in the United States the African American business community was weak. In 1980 the first year that data were adequate to compare minority group businesses, black self-employment stood at 3.3 percent of the over-21 population, while for Hispanics the percentage was 5.5 and for Asians 8.4. In that same year black self-employed income was 20.9 percent lower than that of Hispanics and 31.5 percent less than the self-employed incomes reported by Asians.[9]

No systematic study has as yet appeared to account for the relatively poor performance of the black business sector. Nonetheless Timothy Bates' work has provided important insight into the processes involved. Three variables seem to be important in accounting for differential experiences by ethnic group. In the first place successful entrepreneurship is closely associated with years of educational attainment. The 11.1 years of education reported by blacks in 1980 lagged seriously behind that of nonminority business persons (12.7 years) and even more behind that of Asians (13.6 years), although it was somewhat higher than that reported for Hispanics

(10.6).[10] The second is the industry in which the business is located. The personal services sector in which black business has always been overrepresented is by far the lowest income generating sector of all self-employed industries. The $7,397 reported in that sector in 1980 was 30.5 percent lower than that in all industries and less than half the $15,184 earned in finance, insurance, and real estate—the highest income category.[11] Finally black businesses are chronically underfinanced. Net worth as a percentage of total assets is the statistic Bates employs to measure undercapitalization. In all lines of industry that statistic for minority businesses is 49 percent or less (ranging down to 33.8 percent), whereas for nonminority firms net worth is in excess of 51 percent (ranging up to 56.1 percent). Not surprisingly in light of these figures minority business loan default rates are higher than among nonminority business.[12] The margin for error among black businesses is razor thin because their businesses are starved for financing. A high failure rate is the predictable result.

The poor quality and low level of education received by blacks in the South also acted to limit professional attainment. In 1940 the median years of school completed by African Americans in the South was a mere 5 years; only about 5 percent of the black population had graduated from high school and 1 percent from a college or university. As late as 1947 illiteracy among blacks remained at 11 percent, representing 1.2 million people.[13] These miserable results obviously were the consequence of the lack of need or desire to educate the black population in the plantation economy. What little education was provided was available only in debilitating segregated circumstances. Thus during the 1930–40 academic year, expenditures per black pupil in the South came to $18.82, almost exactly one-third the level spent on that region's white students, which itself was the lowest recorded in the country.[14] It thus is no surprise to learn that in 1940 at the onset of the massive movement to northern cities only 2 percent of African Americans in the South worked as professionals, a number probably exaggerated because it includes individuals in certain categories such as teaching who were not fully credentialed.[15]

With the black business sector hamstrung by its limited access to capital and formal education and with a professional career all but denied to the black population again because of deficiencies in the quality and quantity of education provided to it, economic advance was dependent upon its success in securing employment at relatively high wages or salaries. The difficulty in doing so is indicated in Tables

Table 31   Occupational Distribution of Male Labor Force by Race, 1950–90 (in percentages)

Occupation	1950 Black	1950 White	1970 Black	1970 White	1990 Black	1990 White
Professional and technical	2.2	7.9	7.8	14.6	9.0	15.4
Managers, officials, and proprietors	2.0	11.6	4.7	14.3	6.9	14.5
Clerical	3.4	6.8	7.4	7.1	8.4	5.7
Sales	1.5	6.6	1.8	6.1	5.1	11.9
Craftsmen and foremen	7.6	19.3	13.8	20.8	15.5	20.2
Operatives	20.8	20.0	28.3	18.7	21.8	13.3
Service*	12.5	4.9	12.8	6.0	17.9	8.9
Laborers	23.1	6.6	17.5	6.2	12.7	5.6
Private household	0.8	0.1	0.1	0.3	0.1	—
Farm-related	24.8	14.9	5.3	5.6	2.6	4.5
Not stated	1.3	1.2	0.5	0.3	—	—

Sources: 1950: U.S. Bureau of the Census, *Historical Statistics of the United States, Colonial Times to 1970, Bicentennial Edition*, part I, series D 182-232 (Washington, D.C.: GPO, 1975); 1970: U.S. Department of Labor, Bureau of Labor Statistics, *Handbook of Labor Statistics, 1975—Reference Edition*, bulletin 1865 (Washington, D.C.: GPO, n.d.), table 19; 1990: U.S. Department of Labor, Bureau of Labor Statistics, *Employment and Earnings*, May 1990, vol. 37, no. 5, table A-23.
*Except private household.

31 and 32, which list occupations according to incomes earned. These tables reveal the concentration of black workers in low-income occupations at the time of their massive first entry into the northern industrial economy. Of African American men who were working in 1950, almost one half were employed in the low-income occupations of service, laborers and private household work. By contrast only 13.6 percent of nonfarm white laborers were employed in such low-income jobs. A similar pattern was true for women. Almost half of the black women who were working in 1950 were employed in private household work and the next largest concentration was in services. In contrast, again, white working women were much more evenly distributed over the entire range of occupations.[16] Obviously although the movement to the cities of the North represented occupational advance, it still was the case that the jobs available to African Americans were the least attractive ones generated by the economy. A substan-

Table 32   Occupational Distribution of Female Labor Force by Race, 1950–90 (in percentages)

Occupation	1950		1970		1990	
	Black	White	Black	White	Black	White
Professional and technical	6.2	13.4	10.8	15.0	14.4	19.3
Managers, officials, and proprietors	0.5	4.8	1.9	4.8	7.3	11.6
Clerical	4.0	29.8	20.8	36.4	27.4	28.5
Sales	1.3	8.9	2.5	7.7	9.0	13.4
Craftsmen	1.0	1.7	0.8	1.2	2.4	2.0
Operatives	14.6	19.8	17.6	14.1	9.6	6.5
Service*	17.8	11.4	25.6	15.3	24.1	15.1
Laborers	1.1	0.7	0.7	0.4	1.9	1.5
Private household	42.0	4.4	17.5	3.4	3.5	1.0
Farm	10.8	3.0	0.8	0.7	0.4	1.1
Not stated	0.7	2.1	1.0	1.0	—	—

Source: See Table 31.
*Except private household.

tial degree of additional occupational mobility was required if black poverty were to be escaped.

Tables 31 and 32 reveal that although parity with the white labor force still had not been achieved by 1990, a substantial degree of occupational integration was achieved by the African American labor force. The pattern of upward mobility is particularly obvious among black men in the professional category, where the share of the labor force grew from 2.2 percent in the earlier year to 9.0 percent in 1990. Substantial increases among black men were achieved in other white collar occupations, whereas the low-income occupations that dominated the 1950 pattern all experienced marked declines.

The pattern among African American women is much the same. Most dramatically the concentration of these workers in private household labor has almost completely disappeared. By 1990 more than one-fifth of black women workers were either professionals or managers, while the largest concentration of such individuals occurred in the clerical category. Despite these gains, however, black women in 1990, like their male counterparts, tended to be relatively more concentrated in low-income occupations than was the case among white women in the labor market.

The degree of occupational mobility for African Americans revealed in these tables was determined by three factors. The first was the pace of economic growth experienced by the economy generally. With a high growth rate the demand for labor is strong. Under such circumstances upward black occupational mobility is facilitated by the increase in employment opportunities resulting from such growth. The second factor important in dictating the pace of black occupational mobility has been the rate at which discrimination against African Americans in the labor market was reduced. Obviously the more this occurs the greater the extent of occupational integration no matter what the level of economic and employment growth. The third consideration is the supply of black labor. In particular it is important that as the economy advances and the skill and educational requirements of employment rise, black workers be able to offer the "human capital" employers demand. Thus even if growth were rapid and explicit discrimination effectively eliminated, black workers still might find it difficult to participate effectively in the economy if they lack the credentials demanded by employers.

Of these three factors a significant advance was achieved in promoting occupational integration with the passage of legislation barring racial discrimination in hiring. Title VII of the 1964 Civil Rights Act represents the major victory won by the civil rights movement with regard to employment practices. Under the title a five-member Equal Employment Opportunities Commission (EEOC) was formed to combat discrimination. Over time, the powers of the EEOC were extended to cover even relatively small firms' hiring practices, permitting the commission to initiate suits in federal courts against firms. Related to this was the effect of an Executive Order signed in 1965, which required federal contractors to develop affirmative action programs that had to be approved by the newly created Office of Contract Compliance Programs (OFCCP).[17]

Of course, it is extremely difficult to measure with precision the extent to which this body of antidiscrimination law actually achieved its intended purpose. The problem is that to do so it is necessary to isolate the effects of the legislation from social changes that influenced hiring decisions. Thus, for example, these laws were implemented at a time when attitudes expressed by white people toward African Americans became less hostile.[18] This makes it difficult to know whether the change in the pattern of hiring was the consequence of changed attitudes and would have occurred in the absence of the leg-

Table 33   Average Annual Growth in Real Gross National Product, 1950/60–1980/90 (in percentages)

	1950–60	1960–70	1970–80	1980–90
Growth rate	4.0	4.1	2.8	2.7

Source: Computed from *Economic Report of the President, February 1990*, Annual Report of the Council of Economic Advisors, "Appendix C, Statistical Tables Relating to Income, Employment and Production" (Washington, D.C.: GPO, 1990), table C-5.

islation. However, it is equally plausible that the changed attitudes were the consequence of the laws, and in the absence of the latter the more favorable pattern of employing African Americans would not have occurred. Despite these difficulties of assessment, however, Jaynes and his associates, after reviewing numerous studies on this subject, conclude that "Title VII has had a tremendous effect on behavior in the U.S. labor market." They write:

> Many employers charged with discrimination modified their personnel procedures extensively even before the cases were decided. Other employers altered their procedures after observing companies in their industry being charged with violation of employment discrimination statutes. Major legal changes have occurred in seniority rules, hiring and promotion practices, and even in what constitutes labor market discrimination. . . . These legal changes and their enforcement altered the social context of hiring, firing and promoting. Firms in the private sector as well as local, state and federal governments designed and instituted equal employment policies and affirmative action plans.[19]

Economic expansion also contributed to African American occupational mobility. However the kind of rapid economic growth and therefore employment growth benefitting black labor early in the period was not sustained throughout it. As revealed in Table 33, although the rate of economic growth was robust in the 1950s and 1960s, that pace declined substantially in the following two decades. This decline in growth affected African Americans even more than other workers in the country. This was because blacks had only recently vacated the southern agricultural economy. Having just gained a toehold in the nonagricultural occupational structure, advances for African Americans within that structure required steady and substantial employment growth. However, since soon after the entry of the black labor force into the nonagricultural labor force the pace of

Table 34   Industrial Structure of the Black Labor Force by Sex, 1939–84 (in percentages)

	1939	1949	1959	1969	1979	1984
Men						
Agriculture, forestry, fisheries	42.5	24.9	12.7	5.3	2.8	3.4
Construction, manufacturing, mining	21.8	32.9	35.0	41.3	37.7	33.6
Transportation, communications, public utilities	6.5	9.0	8.2	9.9	12.6	12.6
Wholesale and retail trades	10.1	12.1	13.8	15.1	15.1	16.7
Services	15.8	15.6	17.4	21.1	24.7	27.5
Public administration	1.6	3.9	5.6	7.3	7.0	6.2
Women						
Agriculture, forestry, fisheries	16.1	9.4	3.6	1.4	0.6	0.4
Construction, manufacturing	3.7	9.4	9.3	16.1	18.1	16.5
Transportation, communications, public utilities	0.2	0.9	1.0	3.0	5.2	5.4
Wholesale and retail trades	4.2	10.3	10.1	12.2	12.6	14.3
Services	73.9	65.9	65.0	61.4	55.4	56.5
Public administration	0.6	2.2	3.8	5.9	8.0	6.9

Source: Gerald David Jaynes and Robin M. Williams, Jr. (eds.), *A Common Destiny: Blacks and American Society* (Washington, D.C.: National Academy Press, 1989), p. 273.

expansion decelerated, opportunities for advance were, at least relatively, curtailed.

The slowing of growth is revealed in a change in the industrial employment pattern experienced by the African American labor force after 1969. As indicated in Table 34 between 1939 and 1969 for both men and women the sectors where employment growth was most rapid were the relatively well-paid construction, manufacturing, and mining and public administration industries. For men these two sectors experienced an increase from 23.4 to 48.6 percent between 1939 and 1969. Among black women workers the increase in these sectors was from 4.3 percent to 22.0 percent. In the fifteen years thereafter, however, this pattern was reversed. Among male employees the percentage working in these sectors declined from 48.6 to 39.8 percent between 1969 and 1984; among women there continued to be a slight increase between 1969 and 1979, but a fall occurred thereafter.

Table 35   Median Income of Black Households, 1947–1987
(constant 1987 prices)

Year	Income ($)	Year	Income ($)	Year	Income ($)
1947	6,968	1961	10,257	1975	15,643
1948	7,063	1962	10,587	1976	15,776
1949	6,655	1963	10,883	1977	15,795
1950	7,465	1964	11,899	1978	16,395
1951	7,523	1965	12,172	1979	15,866
1952	8,471	1966	13,900	1980	14,846
1953	8,867	1967	14,722	1981	14,132
1954	8,623	1968	15,350	1982	14,092
1955	9,136	1969	16,406	1983	14,229
1956	9,298	1970	16,206	1984	14,470
1957	9,444	1971	15,653	1985	15,656
1958	9,017	1972	16,132	1986	15,631
1959	10,429	1973	16,585	1987	15,475
1960	10,489	1974	16,050		

Source: 1947–66: U.S. Bureau of the Census, Special Studies, Series P-23, no. 80, *The Social and Economic Status of the Black Population in the United States: An Historical View, 1790–1978* (Washington, D.C.: GPO, n.d.), table 14; the estimates were multiplied by 1.95 to convert constant 1974 prices to constant 1987 prices. 1967–87: U.S. Bureau of the Census, Current Population Reports, Series P-60, no. 162, *Money Income of Households, Families, and Persons in the United States: 1987* (Washington, D.C.: GPO, 1989), table 3.

This change produced a dramatic effect on the pattern of black income growth. As indicated in Table 35 the median income of African American households more than doubled between 1947 and the late 1960s and early 1970s, rising in real terms from about $7,000 to about $16,500. These gains were widely distributed over the population. During these years the percentage of black households earning less than $10,000 declined from 68 percent to 31 percent. At the same time the percentage of such households earning $30,000 or more increased from a mere 2 percent in 1947 to 17 percent (Table 36).

In contrast, however, after the early 1970s these favorable trends came to a halt. The household income level achieved in these years turned out to be peaks not attained again throughout the remainder of the 1970s and the 1980s through 1987 (Table 35). This stagnation in incomes also meant that the decline in the percentage of households earning less than $10,000 was reversed. In the 1980s

Table 36   Black Households Earning under $10,000 and above
$30,000, 1947–87 (constant 1987 prices) (in percentages)

	< $10,000[a]	> $30,000[b]	> $50,000
1947	68	—	—
1953	55	2	—
1959	52	4	—
1964	41	8	—
1969	32	14	5
1973	31	17	6
1978	34	18	7
1983	38	15	6
1987	36	18	8

Sources: 1947–63: U.S. Bureau of the Census, Current Population Reports, Special Studies Series, P-23, no. 80, The Social and Economic Status of the Black Population in the United States: An Historical View, 1790–1978 (Washington, D.C.: GPO, n.d.), table 15; data were multiplied by 1.95 to convert 1974 prices to 1987 prices. 1969–87: U.S. Bureau of the Census, Current Population Reports, Series P-60, no. 162, Money Income of Households, Families, and Persons in the United States: 1987 (Washington, D.C.: GPO, 1989), table 3.
[a]1947–63 less than $9,748.
[b]1947–63 more than $29,250; 1969–87 more than $34,999.

the percentage of such families actually increased from 31 percent in 1973 to 38 percent in 1983 and 36 percent in 1987. Only the very high-income African American households advanced in this period. By 1987, 8 percent of black households were earning $50,000 or more compared to 5 percent in 1969. Thus while the growth experienced between 1947 and 1973 was relatively evenly distributed over the black population, in the years of relatively slow economic growth, low-income households actually saw their income fall, while only the well-to-do experienced income advances.

A similar mixed picture emerges in the African American experience with regard to schooling. Table 37 reports on the years of education to which the United States adult population has been exposed. As is the case with changes in the occupational structure substantial advances for the black population in education have been experienced. By 1988, 26.3 percent of the black population had at least some exposure to college education, a substantial gain from the 10.3 percent level of 1970. Nonetheless it is striking that as recently as 1970 almost 70 percent of adult blacks had not graduated from high

Table 37 Educational Attainment Levels by Race, 1970–88 (in percentages)

	High School		College	
	1–3 years	4 years	1–3 years	4 years
Blacks				
1970	68.6	21.2	5.9	4.4
1980	48.8	29.3	13.5	8.4
1988	36.6	37.1	15.0	11.3
Whites				
1970	45.4	32.2	11.1	11.3
1980	31.2	35.7	16.0	17.1
1988	22.3	39.5	17.2	20.9

Source: U.S. Bureau of the Census, *Statistical Abstract of the United States, 1990* (Washington, D.C.: GPO, 1990), table 216.

school. By 1988 this figure had declined to 36.6 percent. Even so, in that same year there were roughly three times the number of non-high school graduates compared to college graduates among African Americans. Among the adult white population, college graduates approximated the number of non-high school graduates.

The significance of this lag in educational attainment among African Americans is that with economic development the demand for highly educated workers rises. Failure to keep pace with the advancing educational requirements of employment renders a population increasingly vulnerable to setbacks in the labor market. This vulnerability may show up in the form of unemployment. But that is not the only measure which would register a decline in the ability successfully to compete in the labor market. Labor force participation rates—the percentage of the population seeking work—might also decline as individuals become frustrated with their market prospects. Similarly individuals with a low level of skills or education might remain in the market and find work, but also be compelled to accept reduced relative wages. The latter would be the consequence of a decreased demand for poorly educated workers.

There is evidence that in recent years in all three of these measures the relative position of poorly educated African American workers in the United States has declined. Table 38 indicates that between

Table 38   Black Unemployment by Educational Attainment Level,
1977/80–1984/88 (in percentages)

| | High School | | College | |
	1–3 years	4 years	1–3 years	4+ years
1977–80	11.2	9.6	8.2	3.7
1984–88	15.7	12.4	8.8	4.4
Change (%)	40.2	29.2	7.3	18.9

Source: U.S. Bureau of the Census, *Statistical Abstract of the United States, 1990* (Washington, D.C.: GPO, 1990), table 654.

Table 39   Black Labor Force Participation by Educational
Attainment Level, 1970–88 (in percentages)

| | High School | | College | |
	1–3 years	4 years	1–3 years	4+ years
1970	67.1	76.8	81.0	87.4
1975	60.9	75.1	79.7	85.1
1980	58.1	79.2	82.0	90.1
1985	57.0	77.2	85.6	89.9
1988	56.2	77.9	85.5	90.6

Source: U.S. Bureau of the Census, *Statistical Abstract of the United States, 1990* (Washington, D.C.: GPO, 1990), table 627.

1977–80 and 1984–88, two periods of relative prosperity, the unemployment rate for black high school nongraduates increased more than was the case for African Americans with higher levels of educational attainment. It was also the case that the poorly educated suffered with regard to the labor force participation rate. As indicated in Table 39 it was only among those African Americans with less than a high school diploma that the participation rate declined between 1970 and 1988. What seems to have happened is that among blacks who have least been exposed to school, discouragement with job prospects was so intense that large numbers of individuals actually gave up the search for work.

Finally, as indicated in Table 40, the weekly earnings of African Americans with limited education also suffered compared to those

Table 40   Mean Annual Real Income of Blacks by Sex and
Educational Attainment Level, 1969–84 (in dollars)

Years	1969	1979	1984	Change (%)
Males				
8 or less	11,900	13,017	9,957	−16.3
9–11	12,809	11,988	9,127	−28.7
12	15,950	15,313	12,382	−22.4
13–15	17,067	16,648	14,960	−12.3
16+	26,977	25,187	24,175	−10.4
Females				
8 or less	5,440	7,209	6,283	15.5
9–11	6,694	7,782	6,135	−8.4
12	9,307	10,401	9,521	2.3
13–15	11,296	11,566	11,094	−1.8
16+	19,090	17,805	18,592	−2.6

Source: Gerald D. Jaynes, "The Labor Market Status of Black Americans: 1939–1985,"
Journal of Economic Perspectives, vol. 4, no. 4 (Fall 1990), tables 1 and 2.

who were more exposed to formal education. It is true that at each
level of education mean yearly earnings declined for African American men, as well as in three out of five educational categories for
women. Even so the experience was worst for poorly educated men
where the declines ranged between 16 and more than 28 percent. College educated men and all black women did better than that, although
even in these cases reduced yearly incomes occurred—with the ex-
ception of women who had eight or less years of schooling and those
who graduated from high school. The mean yearly income for African
Americans generally fell in this period, but the decline was most dramatic for men who possessed either a high school education or less.

In sum the environment for black economic advance has been
mixed, particularly in the decades of the 1970s and 1980s. Promoting
such growth have been factors such as legal barriers to discrimination
in hiring and the exposure of an increasing fraction of the African
American population to college education. At the same time, however, the decline of the pace of economic growth in the U.S. economy
means that fewer opportunities for advance are being created than
would have been the case if the growth rate of the 1950s and 1960s
had persisted. Furthermore it still is the case that a large fraction of

the black population is barred from highly paid employment—if not in fact by discrimination then because of their limited educational attainment.

The result of these conflicting trends has been a sharp differentiation in economic experience within the African American population. For those who have been exposed to the kind of education required by a modern economy, the legal barring of discrimination in hiring has provided the opportunity for more black occupational mobility than has ever existed in the United States. Indeed, occupational advance for well educated African Americans continued even in the 1970s and 1980s—decades of relatively slow growth. At the same time, however, a large fraction of the black labor force lacks the education to permit it to participate effectively in the contemporary labor market. For them the economic experience of recent years has been devastating, characterized by a steep decline in earnings among the decreasing percentage who have been able to find work. The dynamic of the labor market, then, has produced a divergence in economic experience among African Americans, profoundly differentiating those with the skills and education necessary to participate successfully in the contemporary job market and those who have been deprived of the educational endowment required by employers offering relatively remunerative employment.

These trends toward increased income inequality within the black community look even more ominous in light of recent changes in the structure of the African American family. Since the early 1960s there has been a very large decrease in the marriage rate, an increase in divorce and separation rates, and a substantial decline in the birth rate for legally married African American women, while the birth rate for women who were not legally married has recently increased somewhat. The upshot of these trends has been a major decline in the percentage of black children who reside with two parents. As indicated in Table 41 in 1960 about two out of three African American children resided in two-parent households while that percentage in 1988 was less than two in five.

Single parent families, especially those in which the parent present is a woman (as is true in almost all cases), earn substantially less income than do families in which two parents are present. Thus in 1988 the median income of households in which both parents were present and both employed was $35,276, compared to the $9,710 received in households where the male parent was not present.[20] The

Table 41   Children's Living Arrangements and Births to Legally
Married Women by Race, 1960 and 1988 (in percentages)

	Blacks		Whites	
	1960	1988	1960	1988
Married couple	67.0	38.6	90.9	78.9
Divorced, separated or widowed parent	19.8	24.7	7.1	15.5
Single parent	2.1	29.3	0.1	3.4
Not with a parent	11.1	7.4	1.9	2.2
Births to legally unmarried women	23.3	61.2	2.3	15.7

Source: David T. Ellwood and Jonathan Crane, "Family Change among Black Americans: What Do We Know?" *Journal of Economic Perspectives*, vol. 4, no. 4 (Fall 1990), tables 1 and 2.

effect of the demographic change that has resulted in more African American children living with only one parent combined with the fact that such households receive poverty level incomes is that a majority of black children will spend at least part of their childhood poor.

There are two comments to be made about this pattern of family change and its consequences. First, these changes are not unique to black families in the United States. White families also experienced similar changes during the period since the 1960s. Indeed as David Ellwood and Jonathan Crane report, many of the changes which occurred among white households were proportionately even larger than those among African American households. For example, the proportion of white children who were living in households with one parent rose from 9.1 percent to 21.1 percent, representing a 2.3 fold increase, while the corresponding figures among blacks increased from 33.0 percent to 61.4 percent, representing a 1.9 fold increase (Table 41). Similarly the percentage of white children born to mothers who were legally unmarried increased during these same years from 2.3 percent to 15.7 percent, a 6.8 fold increase. The increase in this statistic for African Americans was from 23.3 percent to 61.2 percent—a 2.3 fold increase (Table 41). Thus it is clear that the dramatic changes in family life in the United States occurred across racial groups, although it is also true that the emergence of single-parent households has developed more among African Americans than among whites.

The second comment is that there is no consensus concerning why these changes have occurred. Ellwood and Crane review three hypotheses offered in this regard: that an increase in welfare benefits is responsible; that the decline in earnings and employment among men accounts for the change; or that the rise in female labor force participation is the causal variable. However, in each case as reported by these authors the evidence is either ambiguous or contrary to the hypothesis; as a result they are able to accept none of them. Instead Ellwood and Crane are drawn to the conclusion that changes in the family in the United States "were generated by a complex interaction of social, cultural, legal and economic factors that will be extremely difficult to disentangle."[21]

In the absence of an adequate theory of family change it would seem unwarranted to assume that the recent trends in family formation patterns will soon alter among either blacks or whites in the United States. Policies therefore to raise living standards will have to work within the new family context rather than anticipating that the pattern of family change will have to be altered in order to stimulate economic advance. Attention therefore must turn to reversing the two factors that appeared most to hinder black economic progress in the 1970s and 1980s: slow economic growth in the country generally, and continued inadequate levels of educational attainment among many African Americans.

The reasons behind the slow rate of economic growth in the United States are complex. At root, however, is that the rate of growth in labor productivity in the 1970s and 1980s was considerably lower than it had been in the 1950s and 1960s. This decline cannot be attributed to a fall in investment. Gross investment rates during these decades actually were higher than they had been in the 1960s.[22] A more likely explanation is that the improvement in the quality of the United States labor force has not kept pace with the requirements associated with modern technology. As a result the pace of productivity growth has slowed. This difficulty becomes all the more stark considering that the growth in the labor force in the future will disproportionately occur among minority members of the population—precisely those who historically have been the least well educated.

These circumstances mean that for now, as was the case in

World War II, the economic interests of white and African American populations have converged. As we have seen for most of their initially imposed residence in the country, African Americans were located in the technological backwater of the South. Indeed their low level of educational attainment actually was functional to that economy; it served to limit their options and effectively helped to confine them to plantation work. After World War II when the exodus from the South reached flood tide, the occupations secured by the new migrants were relatively low-level jobs where education and training once again were neither essential nor necessarily desirable to employers. Now, however, the possession of only limited productive skills by many African American workers may represent a substantial cost to the entire nation. For it seems to represent a major bottleneck to efforts to accelerate national productivity growth. If such an acceleration requires highly educated workers, and minority workers represent a substantial fraction of the labor force of the future, then advancing the educational attainment of such individuals may represent the most effective way for the country to achieve a growth rate consistent with the aspirations of its people. In short, the rejuvenation of U.S. productivity growth may be helped by—indeed, if it is to occur, actually may depend on—a substantial improvement in the level of education secured by African Americans.

Such an increase would, of course, be beneficial to the African American population specifically as well as to the country generally. It would tend to reverse the income polarization which has been experienced within the African American population in recent years. But at the same time such an advance would help to accelerate economic growth in the nation overall. That is, what would be good for the African American population is also what the nation needs. If the condition which must be satisfied for the elimination of disproportionate black poverty is that it be unambiguously in the interests of both blacks and whites, it seems likely that moment has arrived.

Appendix

Number of Counties by State—578

	Total Counties	Plantation Counties
Alabama	67	47
Arkansas	75	23
Georgia	146	70
Louisiana	60	29
Mississippi	79	45
North Carolina	98	21
South Carolina	43	35

Total plantation counties   270
Total nonplantation counties   298

Individual Plantation Counties by State

Alabama (47 counties)

Autauga	Colbert	Jackson	Morgan
Barbour	Coosa	Lauderdale	Perry
Bibb	Crenshaw	Lawrence	Pickens
Bullock	Dale	Lee	Pike
Butler	Dallas	Limeston	Randolph
Calhoun	Dekalb	Lowndes	Russel
Chambers	Elmore	Macon	Sumter
Cherokee	Etowah	Madison	Talladega
Clarke	Greene	Marengo	Tallapoosa
Clay	Hale	Marshall	Tuscaloosa
Cleburne	Henry	Monroe	Wilcox
Coffee	Houston	Montgomery	

Arkansas (23 counties)

Arkansas	Drew	Lincoln	Phillips
Ashley	Hempstead	Little River	Prairie
Chicot	Jackson	Lonoke	Pulaski
Crittenden	Jefferson	Miller	St. Francis
Cross	Lafayette	Mississippi	Woodruff
Desha	Lee	Monroe	

115

Georgia (70 counties)

Baker	Early	Laurens	Schley
Banks	Elbert	Lee	Screven
Bibb	Emanuel	Macon	Stewart
Brooks	Franklin	Madison	Sumter
Bulloch	Grady	Marion	Talbot
Burke	Greene	Meriwether	Taliaferro
Butts	Gwinnett	Miller	Taylor
Calhoun	Hall	Michell	Terrell
Chattachoochee	Hancock	Morgan	Thomas
Clarke	Harris	Muscogee	Troup
Clay	Hart	Newton	Twiggs
Coweta	Henry	Oconee	Walton
Crawford	Houston	Oglethorpe	Washington
Crisp	Jackson	Pulaski	Webster
Decatur	Jasper	Putman	Wilkes
Dodge	Jefferson	Randolph	Worth
Cooly	Jenkins	Rockdale	Quitman
Dougherty	Johnson		

Louisiana (29 counties)

Acadi	East Felicianna	Ouachita	St. Martin
Avoyelles	Iberia	Pointe Coupee	St. Mary
Bossier	Iberville	Rapides	Tensas
Caddo	Lafayette	Red River	West Baton Rouge
Catahoula	Madison	Richland	West Carroll
Concordia	Morehouse	St. Helena	West Feliciana
East Baton Rouge	Natchitoches	St. Landry	Franklin
East Carroll			

Mississippi (45 counties)

Adams	Grenada	Madison	Sharkey
Amite	Hinds	Marshall	Sunflower
Attala	Holmes	Monroe	Tallahatchie
Bolivar	Issaqena	Montgomery	Tate
Carroll	Jefferson	Noxubee	Tunica
Chickasaw	Kemper	Oktibbeha	Union
Claiborne	Lafayette	Panola	Warren
Clay	Lee	Pontotoc	Washington
Coahoma	Leflore	Prentiss	Wilkinson
Copiah	Lincoln	Quitman	Yalobusha
Desota	Lowndes	Rankin	Yazoo
Franklin			

North Carolina (21 counties)

Anson	Halifax	Nash	Scotland
Bladen	Harnett	Pitt	Union
Cumberland	Johnson	Richmond	Wake
Duplin	Lenoir	Robeson	Wayne
Edgecombe	Mecklenburg	Sampson	Wilson
Greene			

South Carolina (35 counties)

Abbeville	Clarendon	Lancaster	Pickens
Aiken	Darlington	Laurens	Richland
Anderson	Dillon	Lee	Saluda
Bamberg	Edgefield	Lexington	Spartanburg
Barnwell	Fairfield	Marion	Sumter
Calhoun	Florence	Marlboro	Union
Cherokee	Greenwood	Newberry	Williamsburg
Chester	Greenville	Oconee	York
Chesterfield	Kershaw	Orangeburg	

Notes

Preface

1. Jay R. Mandle, *The Roots of Black Poverty: The Southern Planta-tion Economy after the Civil War* (Durham: Duke University Press, 1978).
2. See, particularly, William Julius Wilson, *The Declining Significance of Race: Blacks and Changing American Institutions* (Chicago: The University of Chicago Press, 1978), pp. 1–87.

Introduction

1. These data are taken from U.S. Bureau of the Census, Current Population Reports, series P-60, no. 168, *Money Income and Poverty Status in the United States: 1989* (Advance Data from the March 1990 Current Population Survey) (Washington, D.C.: GPO, 1990), tables 1, 2, 17, and 20.
2. Richard A. Easterlin, "Why Isn't the Whole World Developed?" *The Journal of Economic History*, vol. 41, no. 1 (March 1), pp. 1–17.

1 Reestablishing the Plantation Economy

1. Philip D. Curtin, *The Atlantic Slave Trade: A Census* (Madison: University of Wisconsin Press, 1969), table 24, pp. 88–89.
2. Robert William Fogel and Stanley L. Engerman, *Time on the Cross: The Economics of American Negro Slavery* (Boston: Little, Brown and Company, 1974), vol. I, p. 29.
3. Edwin J. Perkins, *The Economy of Colonial America* (New York: Columbia University Press, 1980), p. 71.
4. Karl E. Taeuber and Alma F. Taeuber, "The Negro Population in the United States," in John P. Davis (ed.) *The American Negro Reference Book* (Englewood Cliffs: Prentice-Hall Inc., 1966), p. 98.
5. Computed from Taeuber and Taeuber, "The Negro Population," table I, pp. 106–7.
6. Fogel and Engerman, *Time on the Cross*, vol. I, p. 238.
7. Fogel and Engerman, *Time on the Cross*, vol. I, pp. 70, 90–1, 245.
8. Fogel and Engerman, *Time on the Cross*, vol. I, pp. 255–56.
9. Roger L. Ransom and Richard Sutch, *One Kind of Freedom: The Economic Consequences of Emancipation* (New York: Cambridge University Press, 1977), pp. 52–3.
10. Eric Foner, *Nothing But Freedom: Emancipation and Its Legacy* (Baton Rouge: Louisiana State University Press, 1983), pp. 8–38; Gavin Wright, *Old South, New South: Revolutions in the Southern Economy*

since the Civil War (New York: Basic Books, Inc., 1986), pp. 17–50; Jay R. Mandle, "British Caribbean Economic History: An Interpretation," in Franklin W. Knight and Colin A. Palmer (eds.) *The Modern Caribbean* (Chapel Hill: The University of North Carolina Press, 1989), pp. 231–6.

11. Stanley L. Engerman, "Economic Change and Contract Labour in the British Caribbean: The End of Slavery and the Adjustment to Emancipation," in David Richardson (ed.) *Abolition and its Aftermath: The Historical Context, 1790–1915* (London: Frank Cass, 1985), pp. 225–44; Jay R. Mandle, *The Plantation Economy: Population and Economic Change in Guyana, 1838–1960* (Philadelphia: Temple University Press, 1973), pp. 17–31; Woodville K. Marshall, "Peasant Development in the West Indies since 1838," in P. I. Gomes (ed.) *Rural Development in the Caribbean* (Jamaica: Heinemann Educational Book, 1985), pp. 1–14; Philip J. McLewin, *Power and Economic Change: The Response to Emancipation in Jamaica and British Guiana, 1840–1865* (New York: Garland Publishing Co., 1987), pp. 124–151.

12. George L. Beckford, *Persistent Poverty: Underdevelopment in Plantation Economies of the Third World* (New York: Oxford University Press, 1972), p. 90; Stanley L. Engerman, "Slavery and Emancipation in Comparative Perspective: A Look at Some Recent Debates," *The Journal of Economic History*, vol. XLVI, no. 2, p. 335.

13. Even earlier, in March 1863, some 2,000 acres of land had been purchased collectively by the former slaves on Port Royal, South Carolina. See Willie Lee Rose, *Rehearsal for Reconstruction: The Port Royal Experiment* (New York: Oxford University Press, 1964), pp. 214–15.

14. Claude F. Oubre, *Forty Acres and a Mule: The Freedmen's Bureau and Black Land Ownership* (Baton Rouge: Louisiana State University Press, 1978), pp. 182–4.

15. Eric Foner, *Politics and Ideology in the Age of the Civil War* (New York: Oxford University Press, 1980), pp. 132, 134.

16. W. A. Green, "Was British Emancipation a Success?: The Abolitionist Perspective," in David Richardson (ed.) *Abolition and its Aftermath: The Historical Context, 1790–1916*, p. 186.

17. Foner, *Politics and Ideology*, pp. 132, 143, 144.

18. Christie Farnham Pope, "Southern Homesteads for Negroes," *Agricultural History*, vol. XLIV, no. 2, p. 203.

19. Ibid., pp. 204, 208.

20. Robert Tracy McKenzie, "Postbellum Tenancy in Fayette County, Tennessee: Its Implications for Economic Development and Persistent Black Poverty," *Agricultural History*, vol. 61, no. 2 (Spring 1987), p. 28.

21. According to Gilbert C. Fite in 1900 about 162,000 or 23 percent of black farmers were owners or part owners. This number peaked in 1910 at 195,432. Fite reports that "when it is considered that blacks started out without capital or independent business experience and faced severe racial discrimination, it is not surprising that so few became landowners." Gilbert C. Fite, *Cotton Fields No More: Southern Agriculture 1865–1980* (Lexington: The University Press of Kentucky, 1984), pp. 20–21.

22. Inexplicably both Higgs and Margo in presenting these data (Table 2) emphasize that over the period covered the rate of growth of black wealth exceeded that of white wealth, failing to note that in every case the absolute increase for whites exceeded that of blacks. There is, in short, no evidence whatsoever that the gap between black and white wealth was declining.

23. Stephen J. DeCanio, "Accumulation and Discrimination in the Post-bellum South," in Gary M. Walton and James F. Shepherd (eds.) *Market Institutions and Economic Progress in the New South 1865–1900* (New York: Academic Press, 1981), p. 104.

24. Jonathan M. Wiener, *Social Origins of the New South: Alabama 1860–1885* (Baton Rouge: Louisiana State University Press, 1978), pp. 3–34; Gavin Wright, *Old South, New South*, pp. 17–50; Manning Marable, "The Politics of Black Land Tenure, 1877–1915," *Agricultural History*, vol. 53, no. 1 (1979), pp. 142–52; Higgs, "Accumulation of Property," pp. 725–37.

25. Gail Williams O'Brien, *The Legal Fraternity and the Making of a New South Community, 1848–1882* (Athens, Ga.: The University of Georgia Press, 1986), p. 59.

26. Gerald David Jaynes, *Branches Without Roots: Genesis of the Black Working Class in the American South, 1862–1882* (New York: Oxford University Press, 1986), p. 63

27. Roger Wallace Shugg, "Survival of the Plantation System in Louisiana," *Journal of Southern History*, August 1937, p. 321; See also Rowland T. Berthoff, "Southern Attitudes toward Immigration, 1865–1914," *Journal of Southern History*, August 1951, pp. 326–60; Bert James Loewenberg, "Efforts of the South to Encourage Immigration, 1865–1900," *South Atlantic Quarterly*, October 1934, pp. 364–85.

28. Jaynes, *Branches Without Roots*, p. 313.

29. Joseph D. Reid, Jr., "White Land, Black Labor and Agricultural Stagnation: The Causes and Effects of Sharecropping in the Postbellum South," in Gary M. Walton and James F. Shepherd (eds.) *Market Institutions and Economic Progress in the New South, 1865–1900* (New York: Academic Press, 1981), pp. 36, 47, 43; see also by the same author, "Sharecropping as an Understandable Market Response: The Postbellum South," *The Journal of Economic History*, vol. 33, no. 1, pp. 106–30.

30. Eric Foner, *Reconstruction: America's Unfinished Revolution, 1863–1877* (New York: Harper & Row, 1988), p. 104.

31. Vernon Wharton, *The Negro in Mississippi, 1865–1900* (Chapel Hill: The University of North Carolina Press, 1947), p. 44.

32. Jaynes, *Branches Without Roots*, pp. 220, 221.

33. Jaynes, *Branches Without Roots*, pp. 243–244.

34. August Meier, *Negro Thought in America, 1880–1915* (Ann Arbor: The University of Michigan Press, 1963), p. 44.

35. Ibid., p. 104.

36. Ibid., p. 105.

37. W. E. B. DuBois, "The Negro Landholder of Georgia," *Bulletin of*

the Department of Labor, no. 35 (Washington, D.C.: GPO, 1901), pp. 674–75.

38. Loren Schweninger, *Black Property Owners in the South, 1790–1915* (Urbana and Chicago: University of Illinois Press, 1990), pp. 184, 183.

39. Harold Cruse, "Revolutionary Nationalism and the Afro-American," in James Weinstein and David W. Eakins (eds.) *For a New America: Essays in History and Politics from Studies on the Left, 1959–1967* (New York: Random House, 1970), pp. 355–56.

40. Meier, *Negro Thought in America,* p. 106.

41. W. E. B. DuBois, *The Souls of Black Folk, Essays and Sketches* (Chicago: A. C. McClurg and Company, 1903), pp. 38, 52.

2 The Limits to African American Freedom

1. The 1910 census reported that about one-third of black share tenants had spent one year or less on their current farm. U.S. Bureau of the Census, *Stability of Farm Operations,* unnumbered bulletin (Washington, D.C.: GPO, 1914).

2. Gavin Wright, *Old South, New South: Revolutions in the Southern Economy Since the Civil War* (New York: Basic Books, Inc., 1986), p. 66.

3. Gerald David Jaynes, *Branches Without Roots: Genesis of the Black Working Class in the American South, 1862–1882* (New York: Oxford University Press, 1986), pp. 224–49.

4. Keijiro Otsuka and Yugiro Hayami, "Theories of Share Tenancy: A Critical Survey," *Economic Development and Cultural Change,* vol. 37, no. 1 (October 1988), p. 54.

5. Ronald L. F. Davis, *Good and Faithful Labor: From Slavery to Sharecropping in the Natchez District, 1860–1890* (Westport: Greenwood Press, 1982), p. 179.

6. Pete Daniel, *The Shadow of Slavery: Peonage in the South 1901–1969* (New York: Oxford University Press, 1973), p. 11.

7. Michael Wayne, *The Reshaping of Plantation Society: The Natchez District, 1869–1880* (Baton Rouge: Louisiana State University Press, 1983), pp. 208–9.

8. U.S. Bureau of the Census, Current Population Reports, series P–23, no. 80, *The Social and Economic Status of the Black Population in the United States: An Historical View, 1790–1978,* table 5.

9. By contrast 34.3 percent of the white labor force in these same states was employed in manufacturing and other nonplantation categories. Calculated from Bureau of the Census, Thirteenth Census of the United States, 1910, vol IV, *Occupational Statistics* (Washington, D.C.: GPO, 1914), table VII.

10. Roger L. Ransom and Richard Sutch, *One Kind of Freedom: The Economic Consequences of Emancipation* (New York: Cambridge University Press, 1977), pp. 33–36.

11. Wayne, *The Reshaping of Plantation Society,* p. 195.

12. U.S. Census, 1890, vol. 1, part 2, table 77; U.S. Census 1910, vol. 4, table 10.

13. Wright, *Old South, New South*, pp. 159, 179.

14. Ibid., pp. 177–195.

15. Lance E. Davis, et al. (eds.) *American Economic Growth: An Economist's History of the United States* (New York: Harper & Row, 1972), pp. 138–39; U.S. Bureau of the Census, *Historical Statistics of the United States, Colonial Times to 1970, Bicentennial Edition*, part 1 (Washington, D.C.: GPO, 1975), series F, pp. 287–96.

16. Wright, *Old South, New South*, pp. 74–5.

17. U.S. Bureau of the Census, *Historical Statistics of the United States*, series C89–119, p. 106.

18. Richard Vedder, Lowell Galloway, Philip E. Graves, and Robert Sexton, "Demonstrating their Freedom: The Post-Emancipation Migration of Black Americans," in Paul Uselding (ed.) *Research in Economic History: A Research Annual* (Greenwich: JAI Press, 1986), pp. 218, 219, 220.

19. Ibid., pp. 221–22.

20. Ibid., p. 222 (my emphasis).

21. Davis et al., *American Economic Growth*, p. 137; Brinley Thomas, *Migration and Economic Growth: A Study of Great Britain and the Atlantic Economy*, second edition (Cambridge: Cambridge University Press, 1973), p. 134.

22. For early evidence of an interest in migration see Nell Irwin Painter, *Exodusters: Black Migration to Kansas after Reconstruction* (New York: Alfred A. Knopf, 1977), pp. 184–201.

23. Oscar Zeichner, "The Legal Status of the Agricultural Laborer in the South," *Political Science Quarterly*, vol. 55, no. 3 (September 1940), p. 426.

24. Ibid., p. 428.

25. U.S. Bureau of the Census, *Historical Statistics of the United States*, series C25–75. In contrast, the emigration rate for southern whites increased by about 60 percent.

26. Karl E. Taeuber and Alma F. Taeuber, "The Negro Population in the United States," in John P. Davis (ed.) *The American Negro Reference Book* (Englewood Cliffs: Prentice Hall Inc., 1966), p. 112.

27. Robert Higgs, "Accumulation of Property by Southern Blacks before World War I," *American Economic Review*, vol. 72, no. 4 (September 1982), p. 720; Robert A. Margo, "Accumulation of Property by Southern Blacks before World War I: Comment and Further Evidence," *American Economic Review*, vol. 74, no. 4 (September 1984), p. 770.

28. Robert Higgs, "Race, Skills and Earnings: American Immigrants in 1909," *The Journal of Economic History*, vol. 33, no. 1 (March 1973); Robert Higgs, *The Transformation of the American Economy, 1865–1915* (New York: Wiley, 1971), pp. 115–22.

29. Stanley Lieberson, *A Piece of the Pie: Black and White Immigrants Since 1880* (Berkeley: University of California Press, 1980), pp. 31, 35, 348–49, 369.

30. Theodore Hershberg, Alan N. Burstein, Eugene P. Ericksen, Stephanie W. Greenberg, and William L. Yancy, "A Tale of Three Cities: Blacks, Immigrants and Opportunity in Philadelphia, 1850–1880, 1930, 1970," in Theodore Hershberg (ed.) *Philadelphia: Work, Space, Family and Group Experience in the 19th Century* (New York: Oxford University Press, 1981), pp. 469–70.

3 Tenant Plantation Agriculture

1. Roger L. Ransom and Richard Sutch, *One Kind of Freedom: The Economic Consequences of Emancipation* (New York: Cambridge University Press, 1977), p. 56

2. Roger Wallace Shugg, "Survival of the Plantation System in Louisiana," *Journal of Southern History* (August 1937), p. 311.

3. C. O. Brannen, *Relation of Land Tenure to Plantation Organization*, U.S. Department of Agriculture, Department Bulletin, no. 1269, October 18, 1924, p. 9. In a recent discussion of postbellum plantation agriculture, Nancy Virts concludes that "The amount of cotton produced on tenant plantations in the postbellum period was lower than the percentage of cotton produced on slave plantations of similar size in the antebellum period. But the plantation system and the large-scale cultivation of cotton were still important factors in 1889." Nancy Virts, "Estimating the Importance of the Plantation System to Southern Agriculture in 1880," *The Journal of Economic History*, vol. XLVII, no. 4 (December 1987), p. 988.

4. U.S. Department of Commerce, Bureau of the Census, *Plantation Farming in the United States* (Washington, D.C.: GPO, 1916), pp. 13, 16. Brannen, however, was critical of the selection process. In reviewing the 1910 data he wrote, in 1924, that "some counties containing plantations are not represented in the selected area, and some of the counties represented are only slightly concerned with plantation farming. . . ." C. O. Brannen, *Relation of Land Tenure*, p. 4.

5. Ibid. Tables 11 and 12 are the sources for these calculations.

6. Ibid., p. 2.

7. Gilbert C. Fite, *Cotton Fields No More: Southern Agriculture, 1865–1980* (Lexington: The University Press of Kentucky, 1984), p. 5.

8. C. O. Brannen, *Relation of Land Tenure*, p. 2.

9. Charles S. Johnson, *Statistical Atlas of Southern Counties* (Chapel Hill: The University of North Carolina Press, 1941), p. 15.

10. C. O. Brannen, *Relation of Land Tenure*, pp. 22–23.

11. Warren C. Whatley, "Institutional Change and Mechanization in the Cotton South," *The Journal of Economic History*, vol. XLIV, no. 2 (June 1984), p. 615.

12. C. O. Brannen, *Relation of Land Tenure*, appendix C, table 1.

13. Ibid., p. 30.

14. Charles S. Johnson, Edwin R. Embree, and W. W. Alexander, *The Collapse of Cotton Tenancy, Summary of Field Studies and Statistical Sur-*

veys, 1933–35 (Chapel Hill: The University of North Carolina Press, 1935), pp. 6, 7.

15. Donald Chrichton Alexander, *The Arkansas Plantation, 1920–1942* (New Haven: Yale University Press, 1943), pp. 66–67.

16. C. O. Brannen, *Relation of Land Tenure*, pp. 32, 42.

17. Ibid., p. 29.

18. Ibid., p. 42.

19. Morton Rubin, *Plantation County* (Chapel Hill: The University of North Carolina Press, 1951), pp. 10, 27.

20. Edgar T. Thompson, *Plantation Societies, Race Relations, and the South: The Regimentation of Populations, Selected Papers* (Durham: Duke University Press, 1975), p. 93.

21. Ransom and Sutch, *One Kind of Freedom*, p. 127.

22. H. H. Wooten, *Credit Problems of North Carolina Cropper Farmers*, North Carolina Agricultural Experiment Station, Bulletin 271 (May 1930), cited in T. J. Woofter et al., *Landlord and Tenant on the Cotton Plantation*, Research Monograph 5 (Washington, D.C.: The Division of Social Research, Works Progress Administration, 1936), pp. 61–2.

23. Ransom and Sutch, *One Kind of Freedom*, pp. 130–1.

24. Johnson, Embree, and Alexander, *The Collapse of Cotton Tenancy*, p. 9.

25. Fite, *Cotton Fields No More*, p. 23.

26. Ibid., p. 24. See also Jerome C. Rose, "Biological Consequences of Segregation and Economic Deprivation: A Post-Slavery Population from Southwest Arkansas," *Journal of Economic History*, vol. XLIX, no. 2 (June 1989), pp. 351–60.

4 The Limited Economic Development of the Plantation South

1. See Simon Kuznets, "Modern Economic Growth: Findings and Reflections," in Simon Kuznets, *Population, Capital and Growth* (New York: W. W. Norton and Company Inc., 1973), pp. 165–84.

2. For a discussion of the literature that argues this position, see Harold D. Woodman, "Economic Reconstruction and the Rise of the New South, 1865–1900," in John B. Boles and Evelyn Thomas Nolen (eds.) *Interpreting Southern History: Historiographical Essays in Honor of Sanford W. Higginbotham* (Baton Rouge: Louisiana State University Press, 1987), p. 263–64.

3. Even here, however, the data are grouped by state and do not correspond to the borders of the plantation and nonplantation regions of the South. Nonetheless, the use of data grouped by state allows those states in which plantation agriculture was important to be grouped together and compared with those in which it was not.

4. A similar lag in productivity is reported by Ferleger in the other principal plantation crop, sugar. See Lou Ferleger, "Productivity Change in the Post-Bellum Louisiana Sugar Industry," in O. D. Anderson and M. R.

Perryman (eds.) *Time Series Analysis* (New York: North-Holland Publishing Company, 1981), pp. 147–61.

5. James H. Street, *The New Revolution in the Cotton Economy, Mechanization and Its Consequences* (Chapel Hill: The University of North Carolina Press, 1957), pp. 100–103.

6. Ibid., p. 118.

7. Heywood Fleisig, "Mechanizing the Cotton Harvest in the Nineteenth Century South," *The Journal of Economic History*, vol. 25 (December 1965), p. 704.

8. Gilbert C. Fite, *Cotton Fields No More: Southern Agriculture 1865–1980* (Lexington: University Press of Kentucky, 1984), p. 25. For the experience in sugar see Lou Ferleger, "Farm Mechanization in the Southern Sugar Sector after the Civil War," *Louisiana History*, vol. XXIII, no. 1 (winter 1982), pp. 21–34.

9. William M. Parker, "Agriculture," in Lance Davis et al. (eds.) *American Economic Growth, An Economist's History of the United States* (New York: Harper and Row, 1972), p. 385.

10. Jacob Schmookler, *Invention and Economic Growth* (Cambridge: Harvard University Press, 1966), p. 206.

11. Warren C. Whatley, "Southern Agrarian Labor Contracts as Impediments to Cotton Mechanization," *The Journal of Economic History*, vol. XLVII, no. 1 (March 1987), pp. 51–2.

12. William Parker, "Agriculture," pp. 395, 396.

13. Gavin Wright, *Old South, New South: Revolutions in the Southern Economy since the Civil War* (New York: Basic Books, Inc., 1986), p. 79.

14. Lance E. Davis, "The Investment Market, 1870–1914: The Evolution of a National Market," *The Journal of Economic History*, vol. 25, no. 3 (September, 1965), pp. 388–92.

15. The issue of capital goods is taken up in Lou Ferleger, "Capital Goods and Southern Economic Development," *Journal of Economic History*, vol. XLV, no. 2 (June 1985), pp. 411–17.

5 The Plantation Economy

1. Eric Foner, *Reconstruction: America's Unfinished Revolution, 1863–1877* (New York: Harper & Row, 1988), pp. 291, 333.

2. Gail Williams O'Brien, *The Legal Fraternity and the Making of a New South Community, 1848–1882* (Athens, Ga.: The University of Georgia Press, 1986), pp. 58–75.

3. Robert Higgs, *Competition and Coercion: Blacks in the American Economy, 1865–1914* (New York: Cambridge University Press, 1977), p. 124.

4. See Ulrich Bonnell Phillips, *The Slave Economy of the Old South: Selected Essays in Economic and Social History*, edited and with an introduction by Eugene D. Genovese (Baton Rouge: Louisiana State University Press, 1968), pp. 245, 267.

5. Edgar T. Thompson, *Plantation Societies, Race Relations and the*

South: The Regimentation of Populations (Durham: Duke University Press, 1975), p. 242.

6. Ibid., p. 86.

7. Ibid., pp. 33, 36–39.

8. Eugene D. Genovese, "On Antonio Gramsci," in Eugene D. Genovese (ed.) *In Red and Black: Marxian Explorations in Southern and Afro-American History* (New York: Vintage Books, 1971), p. 406.

9. Eugene D. Genovese, *Roll, Jordan, Roll: The World the Slaves Made* (New York: Pantheon Books, 1974), pp. 5–7.

10. Ibid., p. 661.

11. Ibid., p. 111.

12. James Larry Roark, "Masters without Slaves: Southern Planters in the Civil War and Reconstruction," Ph.D. dissertation, Stanford University, 1973, p. 321.

13. Ibid., pp. 323, 327.

14. Michael Wayne, *The Reshaping of Plantation Society: The Natchez District, 1860–1880* (Baton Rouge: Louisiana State University Press, 1983), p. 202.

15. Gunnar Myrdal, *An American Dilemma, The Negro Problem and Modern Democracy* (New York: Harper and Brothers, 1944), pp. 459, 593.

16. Arthur F. Raper, *Preface to Peasantry: A Tale of Two Blackbelt Counties* (Chapel Hill: The University of North Carolina Press, 1936), p. 122.

17. W. T. Couch, "The Negro in the South," in W. T. Couch (ed.) *Culture in the South* (Chapel Hill: The University of North Carolina Press, 1936), p. 122.

18. Richard Wright, *Black Boy: A Record of Childhood and Youth* (New York: Harper & Row, 1945), p. 253.

19. Lee J. Alston and Joseph P. Ferrie, "Social Control and Labor Relations in the American South Before the Mechanization of the Cotton Harvest in the 1950s," *Journal of Institutional and Theoretical Economics*, vol. 145, no. 1 (March 1989), p. 134.

20. Ibid., pp. 136, 137.

21. Lee J. Alston, "Race Etiquette in the South: The Role of Tenancy," in Paul Uselding (ed.) *Research in Economic History: A Research Annual* (Greenwich: JAI Press, 1986), vol. 10, pp. 200, 201.

22. Allison Davis, Burleigh B. Gardner, and Mary R. Gardner, *Deep South: A Social and Anthropological Study of Caste and Class* (Chicago: University of Chicago Press, 1941), pp. 43–44.

23. James Elbert Cutler, *Lynch-Law: An Investigation into the History of Lynching in the United States* (original edition, 1905; reprinted, Montclair: Patterson Smith, 1969), p. 179.

24. Thompson, *Plantation Societies*, p. 86.

25. Barbara Jeanne Fields, "Advent of Capitalist Agriculture: The New South in a Bourgeois World," in Thavolia Glymph and John J. Kushma (eds.) *Essays on the Postbellum Southern Economy* (College Station, Tex.: Texas A & M Press, 1985), p. 74; Harold D. Woodman, "The Reconstruc-

tion of the Cotton Plantation in the New South," in Glymph and Kushma (eds.), *Postbellum Southern Economy*, p. 99.

26. Fields, "Advent of Capitalist Agriculture," p. 74; Woodman, "Reconstruction of the Cotton Plantation," pp. 113, 100.

6   Leaving the South

1. Edward F. Denison, *Accounting for United States Economic Growth, 1929–1969* (Washington, D.C.: The Brookings Institution, 1974), pp. 62–64.

2. U.S. Bureau of the Census, *Historical Statistics of the United States, Colonial Times to 1970, Bicentennial Edition, Part 1*, series C25-73 (Washington, D.C.: GPO, 1975).

3. Daniel M. Johnson and Rex R. Campbell, *Black Migration in America: A Social Demographic History* (Durham: Duke University Press, 1981), p. 72. See also Kent Osband, "The Boll Weevil versus King Cotton," *Journal of Economic History*, vol. XLV, no. 3 (September 1985), pp. 627–43.

4. Reynolds Farley, *Growth of the Black Population: A Study of Demographic Trends* (Chicago: Markham Publishing Company, 1971), pp. 46–7.

5. Neil R. McMillen, *Dark Journey: Black Mississippians in the Age of Jim Crow* (Urbana and Chicago: University of Illinois Press, 1989), p. 264.

6. Richard A. Easterlin, "The American Population," in Lance E. Davis et al. (eds.) *American Economic Growth: An Economist's History of the United States* (New York: Harper & Row, 1972), p. 137.

7. James R. Grossman, *Land of Hope: Chicago, Black Southerners, and the Great Migration* (Chicago and London: The University of Chicago Press, 1989), pp. 19, 59, 60, 261; W. E. B. DuBois, "Brothers, Come North," *Crisis*, vol. 19, no. 3 (January 1920), pp. 105–6.

8. Grossman, *Land of Hope*, p. 79; quoted in Roi Ottley, *The Lonely Warrior: The Life and Times of Robert S. Abbott* (Chicago: Henry Regnery Company, 1955), p. 160.

9. Florette Henri, *Black Migration: Movement North, 1900–1920* (Garden City: Anchor Press/Doubleday, 1972), p. 64.

10. Grossman, *Land of Hope*, pp. 87–8.

11. Ibid., p. 84–5.

12. William Julius Wilson, *The Declining Significance of Race: Blacks and Changing American Institutions* (Chicago and London: The University of Chicago Press, 1978), p. 72.

13. Thomas Sowell, *Race and Economics* (New York: David McKay Company Inc., 1975), p. 120.

14. Amy Jacques-Garvey (ed.), *Philosophy and Opinions of Marcus Garvey* (New York: Atheneum, 1969), vol. I, p. 38.

15. Harold Cruse, "Revolutionary Nationalism and the Afro-American," in James Weinstein and David W. Eakins (eds.) *For a New America:*

Essays in History and Politics from Studies on the Left, 1959–1967 (New York: Random House, 1970), p. 357.

16. Elton C. Fax, *Garvey: The Story of a Pioneer Black Nationalist* (New York: Dodd, Mead and Company, 1972), pp. 145–46.

17. Jacques-Garvey, *Philosophy and Opinions*, vol. I, p. 39.

18. Robert L. Allen, *Black Awakening in Capitalist America: An Analytic History* (Garden City: Doubleday and Company Inc., 1970), p. 102.

19. T. J. Woofter noted the beginning of just such changes as early as 1916–17. See his *Negro Migration, Changes in Rural Organization and Population of the Cotton Belt* (New York: AMS, 1971 [1920]), pp. 157–67.

20. U.S. Bureau of the Census, *Historical Statistics of the United States*, series C25–73.

21. The relief statistics are taken from Raymond Walters, *Negroes and the Great Depression, The Problem of Economic Recovery* (Westport: Greenwood Publishing Corporation, 1970), p. 91; Mary Ellison, *The Black Experience: American Blacks since 1865* (New York: Barnes and Noble, 1974), p. 123.

22. Arnold Rose, *The Negro in America* (New York: Harper and Brothers, 1948), pp. 120–21.

23. Warren C. Whatley, "Labor for the Picking: The New Deal in the South," *The Journal of Economic History*, vol. XLIII, no. 4 (December, 1983), p. 914; see also Gavin Wright, *Old South, New South: Revolutions in the Southern Economy since the Civil War* (New York: Basic Books, Inc., 1986), p. 228.

24. David Eugene Conrad, *The Forgotten Farmers: The Story of Sharecroppers in the New Deal* (Urbana: University of Illinois Press, 1965), pp. 43–44.

25. Whatley, "Labor for the Picking," pp. 915–16.

26. Gunnar Myrdal, *An American Dilemma: The Negro Problem and Modern Democracy* (New York: Harper and Brothers, 1944), p. 253.

27. Nicholas Lemann, *The Promised Land: The Great Black Migration and How it Changed America* (New York: Alfred A. Knopf, 1991), pp. 14–15.

28. Ellison, *Black Experience*, pp. 114–15.

29. Theodore Rosengarten, *All God's Dangers: The Life of Nate Shaw* (New York: Alfred A. Knopf, 1974), pp. 296–309.

7 The Collapse of the Plantation Economy

1. U.S. Bureau of the Census, *Historical Statistics of the United States, Colonial Times to 1970, Bicentennial Edition, Part 1*, series C25–75 (Washington, D.C.: GPO, 1975).

2. U.S. Department of Labor, *Crops and Markets* (January 1946), p. 45.

3. "War and Post-War Trends in Employment of Negroes," *Monthly Labor Review* (January 1945), p. 4.

4. Mary Ellison, *The Black Experience: American Blacks since 1865* (New York: Barnes and Noble, 1974), p. 148.

5. Ibid., pp. 149–53.

6. Quoted in Robert C. Weaver, *Negro Labor, A National Problem* (New York: Harcourt, Brace and Company, 1946), p. 27.

7. Abram J. Jaffe and Seymour Wolfbein, "Post-War Migration Plans of Army Enlisted Men," *The Annals*, vol. 238 (March 1945), pp. 18–26.

8. "War and Post-War Trends," p. 5.

9. Nancy Virts argues that as late as 1945 the tenant plantation system allowed planters to achieve economies of scale in marketing high-quality cotton. Nancy Virts, "The Efficiency of Southern Tenant Plantations, 1900–1945," *Journal of Economic History*, vol. 51, no. 2 (June 1991), pp. 385–95.

10. Seymour Melman, "An Industrial Revolution in the Cotton South," *Economic History Review*, second series, vol. II, no. 1 (1949), p. 64.

11. Gavin Wright, *Old South, New South: Revolutions in the Southern Economy since the Civil War* (New York: Basic Books Inc., 1986), pp. 241–42.

12. Warren C. Whatley, "Southern Agrarian Labor Contracts as Impediments to Cotton Mechanization," *Journal of Economic History*, vol. XLVII, no. 1 (March 1987), pp. 64–68.

13. James Street, *The New Revolution in the Cotton Economy: Mechanization and Its Consequences* (Chapel Hill: The University of North Carolina Press, 1957), pp. 129–30.

14. U.S. Department of Agriculture, Bureau of Agricultural Statistics, Statistical Bulletin, no. 99, *Statistics on Cotton and Related Data* (Washington, D.C.: GPO, June 1951).

15. Willis Peterson and Yoav Kislev, "The Cotton Harvester in Retrospect: Labor Displacement or Replacement?" *Journal of Economic History*, vol. XLVI, no. 1 (March 1986), pp. 199–216.

8   Limited Economic Integration

1. U.S. Bureau of the Census, *Historical Statistics of the United States, Colonial times to 1970, Bicentennial Edition Part 1*, series A 172–194 and A73–81 (Washington, D.C.: GPO, 1975); U.S. Bureau of the Census, *The Social and Economic Status of the Black Population in the United States, 1790–1978*, Current Population Reports, Special Studies, series P-23, no. 80, tables 5, 6, and 8.

2. Mary Ellison, *The Black Experience: American Blacks since 1865* (New York: Barnes and Noble, 1974), p. 183. See also Howell Raines, *My Soul is Rested: The Story of the Civil Rights Movement in the Deep South* (New York: G. P. Putnam's Sons, 1977).

3. Gerald David Jaynes and Robin M. Williams, Jr. (eds.), *A Common Destiny: Blacks and American Society* (Washington, D.C.: National Academy Press, 1989), p. 221.

4. Ibid., p. 221.

5. Richard Wright, *12 Million Black Voices: A Folk History of the Negro in the United States* (New York: Viking, 1941), p. 93.

6. Data in the following two paragraphs are computed from Sar A. Levitan and Robert Taggert, *Still a Dream: The Changing Status of Blacks since 1960* (Cambridge: Harvard University Press, 1975), pp. 28–31.

7. Joseph Pierce, *Negro Business and Business Education* (New York: Harper and Brothers, 1947), pp. 15–35.

8. Timothy Bates, "An Analysis of Black Entrepreneurship," Preliminary report to the Panel on Employment, Income, and Occupations, National Academies of Sciences (Mimeo, n.d.), p. 23.

9. Timothy Bates, "Self-Employed Minorities: Traits and Trends," *Social Science Quarterly*, vol. 68, no. 3 (September 1987), p. 544.

10. Ibid., p. 544.

11. Timothy Bates, "Entrepreneur Human Capital Endowments and Minority Business Viability," *The Journal of Human Resources*, vol. XX, no. 4 (1985), p. 544.

12. Timothy Bates, "Impact of Preferential Procurement Policies on Minority-Owned Business," *The Review of Black Political Economy*, vol. 14, no. 1 (Summer 1985), pp. 59–61.

13. U.S. Bureau of the Census, *The Social and Economic Status of the Black Population*, tables 70 and 68.

14. Jaynes and Williams, *A Common Destiny*, p. 59. For a detailed examination of this subject see Robert A. Margo, *Race and Schooling in the South, 1880–1950* (Chicago: The University of Chicago Press, 1990).

15. U.S. Bureau of the Census, *The Social and Economic Status of the Black Population*, table 54.

16. These estimates are obtained by subtracting the percentage of the labor force in agriculture from 100 then dividing the share of the labor force in a specific sector by the result.

17. Jaynes and Williams, *A Common Destiny*, pp. 316–17.

18. Mildred A. Schwartz, *Trends in White Attitudes toward Negroes*, report no. 119 (Chicago: National Opinion Research Center, The University of Chicago, 1967), pp. 1–50.

19. Jaynes and Williams, *A Common Destiny*, p. 319.

20. U.S. Bureau of the Census, Current Population Reports, series P-20, no. 442, *The Black Population in the United States: March 1988* (Washington, D.C.: GPO, 1989), table 9.

21. David T. Ellwood and Jonathan Crane, "Family Change Among Black Americans: What Do We Know?" *Journal of Economic Perspectives*, vol. 4, no. 4 (Fall 1990), p. 81.

22. Lou Ferleger and Jay R. Mandle, "Reverse the Drain on Productivity with Mass Education and Retraining," *Challenge*, vol. 33, no. 4 (July/August 1990), pp. 19–20.

Index

Abbott, Robert, 71
abolitionists: English goals, 9
acreage: landlord farms, 36; tenant
  farms, 36
Adams County (Miss.), 23
Africa, 5, 73, 74
African American(s): businesses, 15,
  19, 72, 99, 100; children's living arrangements, 111, 112; community
  organizations, 96; confinement to
  South, 68; deference, 22; deference
  and landownership, 61–62; economic differentiation, 111; education, 3, 100, 107–8, 110, 111, 114;
  electoral disenfranchisement, 19,
  58; entrepreneurial experience, 18,
  72, 94, 99; family, 111, 113; farm
  owners, 17; geographic concentration, 23; geographic distribution, 1,
  3; household incomes, 1, 16, 106,
  107, 110, 111; incomes (Chicago),
  80; incomes (New York), 80; incomes (the North), 78; information
  about the North, 29, 30; integrationist politics, 74, 75; landownership, 11, 12, 16, 17, 18, 24, 31;
  life-styles, 98; market, 18; migration from the South, 1, 3, 25–30,
  69–71, 75–78, 81, 84, 88–90, 93,
  95–96, 98; migration plans (post-
  WWII), 88; nationalism, 73–74;
  opposition to migration from
  South, 70; ownership of wealth,
  98–99; politics during Reconstruction, 58; poverty, 18, 43, 44, 57,
  77, 84; support for the New Deal,
  75; tensions with white working
  class, 72. See also African American labor
African American labor: demand for,
  2, 21, 23, 24, 25, 28, 30, 31, 32, 33,
  38, 68, 69, 71, 72, 75–78, 80, 81–
  82, 84, 85–87, 88–90, 93, 94, 95,
  96, 97, 101–5, 110, 111, 114; dis-

crimination against, 24–25, 28, 30–
  32, 68, 72, 88, 93, 96–98, 110, 111;
  employment during WWII, 87;
  freedom, 21–23; immobility, 68;
  industrial distribution, 105; occupations, 23, 24, 101–3, 114; participation rate, 109; skills, 93, 98, 103;
  unemployment, 109; wages in the
  North, 30, 31
Agricultural Adjustment Act (AAA),
  80, 81, 89
Alabama, 6, 17, 24, 29, 30, 34, 35, 36,
  46, 47, 53, 78, 82
Alexander, David, 40
Allis Chalmers Manufacturing Co., 91
Alston, Lee J., 63, 64
antienticement and antirecruitment
  legislation, 29
Arkansas, 17, 24, 34, 35, 36, 46, 47,
  64, 78
Asian businesses, 99

Barbados, 8
Barton, Glen T., 48
Bates, Timothy, 99
black nationalism, 19
"black belt," 36; self determination,
  74
boll weevil infestation, 50
Brannen, C. O., 33, 36, 38, 39, 40, 41
Brodell, Albert P., 48
*Brown v. The Board of Education of
  Topeka*, 97

capital goods, 52
capitalism, 66
capital markets, 56
Caribbean: survival of plantation
  cultivation, 8
cash renters, 39
Chicago Defender, 71
Chinese: immigrants to U.S. South,
  13
CIO, 88

About the Author

Jay R. Mandle is the W. Bradford Wiley Professor of Economics at Colgate University and the author of *Roots of Black Poverty: The Southern Plantation Economy after the Civil War* (Duke University Press, 1978).

Library of Congress Cataloging-in-Publication Data

Mandle, Jay R.
    Not slave, not free : the African American economic
experience since the Civil War / Jay R. Mandle.
        p.   cm.
    Includes bibliographical references and index.
    ISBN 0-8223-1172-0 (acid-free paper)
    ISBN 0-8224-1220-4 (pbk.)
    1. Afro-Americans—Economic conditions.   2. Afro-
Americans—History.   I. Title.
E185.M18   1992
330.973'0089'96073—dc20   91-27995
                                                     CIP